ER

SWAN
SINKS

ISLAND BOOKS
Westport, Connecticut

Swan Sinks:
S.S. *Cygnet* Sunk by Italian Submarine, *Enrico Tazzoli* San Salvador, Bahamas in World War II

Eric Wiberg

For my siblings; Ann, John & James

by the same author:
U-Boats off Bermuda
U-Boats in the Bahamas
Round the World in the Wrong Season
Tanker Disasters
Published Writing
Juvenilia
Pending:
U-Boats in New England,
Mailboats of Bahamas,
Drifting to the Duchess

Published by Island Books, Westport, CT, USA
Copyright © Eric Troels Wiberg, 2017, ericwiberg.com

All rights reserved. No part of this publication may be reproduced in any manner or by any means without the prior written permission of the publisher except in the case of brief quotations embodied in articles or reviews. To contact the author email eric@ericwiberg.com.

ISBN: # 978-0-9843998-8-8 / 0-9843998-8-7
Library of Congress Control Number: 2017905764
Printed in the United States of America
First Edition, Island Books, 2017

CONTENTS

	Introduction	
1.	Carlo Fecia di Cossato & R.Smg. *Enrico Tazzoli,* Early Careers	01-12
2.	S.S. *Cygnet,* History, Owners, & Charterers	13-22
3.	*Cygnet*'s Officers & Men	*23-29*
4.	*Cygnet*'s Final Voyage	31-33
5.	Attack, March 11th 1942	35-49
6.	San Salvador to Nassau, *Monarch of Nassau*, March 12-13 1942	51-54
7.	Nassau, Bahamas, March 1320, 1942	55-64
8.	Transport to Miami & New York, March 20-23, 1942	65-70
9.	*Enrico Tazzoli,Daytonian&Athelqueen*, March 12-15, 1942	71-80
10.	S.S. *Davila*Attacked by *Enrico Tazzoli,* March 20, 1942	81-85
11.	DiCossato, Career and Suicide, Following *Enrico Tazzoli*	87-90
12.	Postscript: Fates of *Cygnet* Officers, Men& Vessels	91-104
	Conclusion	105-110
	Resources	111-114
	Appendices	115-119
	Acknowledgments	121-122
	About the Author	123

INTRODUCTION

In a little-known theater of war where 130 Allied ships were sunk by 112 German and Italian submarines, almost all of them in the spring of 1942, the loss of the Greek-owned steam ship, *Cygnet,* to the Italian submarine *Enrico Tazzoli,* is remarkable on many levels. For one, no one was killed, or even seriously injured, and, in fact, the Italians and Greeks both saluted and joked with one another during and after the attack. Considering that 5,844 Allied sailors were attacked in the Bahamas area, and that 1,239 of them were killed, this is remarkable. Also *Cygnet* was the only ship in the Bahamas or Turks & Caicos whose sinking was so close to land San Salvador was less than six miles away that local Bahamians witnessed the daytime assault and the district commissioner sent out an SOS to the government forces calling for a counter-attack.

Cygnet was only the second Allied ship sunk in the Bahamas during the war, the only Greek-owned vessel (the owners still maintain close shipping ties to the Bahamas), and the first to be dispatched by an Italian submarine. The *O.A. Knudsen* of Norway was caught between Abaco and Eleuthera two days before, and the *Tazzoli* sank the British steamers *Daytonian* and *Athelqueen*, in that area several days later. All of the other ships sunk in the Bahamas left dead sailors behind; trapped on the ships, buried at sea, lost on the reefs, or buried ashore. A fortunate 257 of them made it to the welcome safety of Nassau and into the waiting arms of the Duchess of Windsor, Wallis Simpson, and her Red Cross volunteers.

The attack on the *Cygnet* in Bahamian waters was a shock on many levels. The 1939 Declaration of Panama established a neutrality zone extending 300 nautical miles from US territories, prohibiting the warships of belligerent nations from entering it. This, of course, was pierced after Adolf Hitler declared war on the United States in December 1941, a few days after Pearl Harbor. Still, the Americans and their Allies in the Bahamas and other Caribbean colonies were not expecting German or Italian attacks that first winter. Nor, by any objective standard, were they prepared for them (a situation resulting in a blame game derisively called the Battle of Washington).

Whereas the rumor that an Axis submarine shelled Mona Island between Hispaniola and Puerto Rico on March 3, were unfounded, the historical record is replete with multiple attacks much more alarming; starting with that on the *Cygnet* a week later. Italian submarines amassed half-a-dozen patrols east of the Bahamas and penetrated the Caribbean Sea to the coast off Aruba. German U-boats attacked the sea-lanes off the Panama Canal, causing such a stir that two Allied subs the *Dorado* and the French *Surcouf* - were sunk by friendly fire. No Italian submarine approached as close to the coast of the United States as the *Tazzoli*, which chose to return home between Bermuda and the US mainland.

Had it not been disabled at the time, history might have paid more attention. As it was, the submarine returned to Europe, its exploits relatively unknown to the Allies, and was sunk soon thereafter.

Meanwhile the Italian's German colleagues mined most of the ports between Boston and San Juan, including in the US Gulf. They landed saboteurs in Florida, New York, Maine, New Brunswick, and the Gulf of Saint Lawrence. In fact, German and Italian submarines penetrated the Red Sea, the Persian Gulf, Indonesia, the Pacific, Australia, and even New Zealand. Early in the war their surface raiders captured a Norwegian whaling fleet in the Antarctic and navigated the Arctic route from the Atlantic to the Pacific oceans. The question with respect to German and Italian submarines was not so much what they did, but what they *didn't* manage to do and where they didn't manage to go.

Betasom was a German and Italian joint venture, resulting from the Italians having, at one point in the war, the largest fleet of submarines in the world. The Germans wanted it to fulfil Admiral Karl Dönitz's and Hitler's vision of domination of the seas. Britannia may have ruled the waves, but beneath them the Axis controlled the battle, at least until Black May of 1943, when Allies turned the tides and Dönitz recalled his wolf packs. As one German sub-commander wryly put it, he worked for the largest ship-scrapping effort in world history. The Germans alone accounted for 2,779 vessels and over 14 million gross registered tons of Allied shipping sent to the bottom. During 1942 they destroyed over six million tons.

The Axis' goals in the Western Hemisphere were two-fold: to cut off the supply of oil (tankers) from the US Gulf and Venezuela to Halifax, where it was being protectively convoyed to the UK, and to sink Allied ships faster than they could rebuild them. They very nearly succeeded, since in the winter of 1942 (Operation Drumbeat off the US east coast) and in the spring of 1942 (Operation *Neuland*, in the Caribbean) they were sinking an average of a tanker every 10 hours.

Due of a lack of convoys, escorts, air cover, and signals intelligence, coupled with lights including lighthouses blazing from shore, German and Italian commanders would actually choose which type of ship to expend the valuable torpedoes on. They could afford not only to let the smaller prey pass, but also to linger at the site of an attack for hours, to both ensure that the victim was finished off and to interact with the survivors, gain intelligence, and provide assistance if needed. It was indeed, a fairly unique theatre of war in that regard, to the extent that Germans called early 1942 the second happy time, recalling the outbreak of war, when pickings were relatively easy and safe.

As for sinking more ships than Allies could replace, the Germans made stellar progress from September 1939 to spring of 1943, but then improved intelligence, detection, sub-sea bombing techniques, sonar, hunter-killer groups, the elimination of supply U-boats, and improvements in the range, capacity, and sub-detection capabilities (radar and Leigh lights) on airplanes, sealed their doom, finally with the closing of the air gap over the North Atlantic between Canada and Europe.

The nail in the Axis' coffin was the mass-production by American industrialists like Henry J. Kaiser of the *Liberty Ship*, a wonder of assembly-line output, resulting in ships being launched less than a week after having their keels being laid, a feat not achieved before or since. This was all made easier by a workforce sheltered from the war, access to raw materials such as the bauxite and iron ore which ships like the *Cygnet* carried to the US, nationalization of shipyards by the Maritime Administration, and a keen workforce, much of it supplemented by women.

The human element of a relatively small incident like the loss of the relatively small, 3,530-ton*Cygnet*, is both compelling and illustrative of the larger, global struggle. The ship itself had served the US government in World War I, and had run between Europe and South America for decades. Built Dutch, she was owned and crewed mostly Greek, flagged to Panama, and trading for Canadians to and from South America and the Caribbean. Though the owners had a contract (charter party) stating no deck-cargo was to be carried, a young Bahamian boy and his family retrieved bales of rubber that floated free after the sinking. The *Cygnet* men were the only Allied sailors rescued by the *Monarch of Nassau*, though on another Bahamian vessel, the *Ena K.*, they shared space with survivors of other shipwrecks, and missed sailing with Sydney Poitier by mere weeks.

The attack itself was recorded for posterity, live by the Italians, so that we can watch it online even whilst on the move ourselves. The crew was mostly from small islands in the Greek archipelago (only two out of 28 Greeks were from Athens, and most were from Andros or Chios).A pair were also from Romania and Spain. They were able to interact with their Italian attackers for roughly an hour, then encounter a one-legged white man in a rowboat who guided them between the reefs at 4 am, then accept a ride from Captain Roland Roberts aboard his British-built freighter, before meeting the Duke and Duchess of Windsor in the colony's capital, Nassau. Overall, the men would travel by lifeboat, lorry, passenger ship, a motor sailor, and train over two weeks before they reached a base, albeit in exile.

In Nassau the sailors were given an open-armed welcome from fellow Greeks from Kalymnos, living industriously in the Bahamas since the late 1800s, when they had arrived for the prosperous sponge fishing trade, which had recently collapsed. They shared the island and no doubt the pubs with over 100 other cast-up sailors from other vessels. From there Captain Charles A. Pettee, master of a wooden freighter built in Harbour Island that was overcrowded with castaways and farmers took them to the US. They were cleared outwards by two American consuls from Minnesota, and interviewed by US Navy intelligence officers before being reunited with their employers in New York. They too, had been forced by the war to move from Andros to Athens, London, and then to New York. For most of the sailors, it would take years, until the war's end, before they would beable to reunite with their friends and family in Greece. Some of them would opt to stay in America, because of the *Cygnet*.

The loss of the *Cygnet* gave the men, on both sides of the steel vessels involved,plenty to photograph and film, talk and write about, and remember. There is a certain irony in the

Cygnet skipper's letter of protest, filed in Nassau, where men on both sides admit that interactions between Italians and Greek were jocular and relaxed. Interestingly, it was the Greek, and not the Italian sailors, who lived to tell the tale. Within a year the *Tazzoli*, too, was at the sea floor; her commander dead by his own hand and his legacy only resurrected with an Italian submarine named after him, generations later.

Chapter 1

CARLO FECIA DI COSSATO & R.SMG. *ENRICO TAZZOLI*

The *Enrico Tazzoli* was one of three submarines of the *Calvi* class, so named after the first submarine in the series, the *Pietro Calvi*. Launched on October 14th, 1935, the submarine was named after a martyr of the Italian wars of independence. The other *Calvi* class boats were the *Giuseppe Finzi* and *Tazzoli*. All three were built by the Oderno-Terni-Orlando shipyard in Genoa, were initially deployed in the Mediterranean and then patrolled to the greater Bahamas area during the war the *Finzi* twice. The design of the submarine was of civilian origin. Submarines after this were designed by the naval draftsmen in the *Regia Marina*, or the Royal Navy of Italy. They were designed for blue-water, or ocean-going operations in the open sea, and the salient feature was double hull throughout.

CARLO FECIA DI COSSATO & R.SMG. ENRICO TAZZOLI

Royal Italian Navy submarine, R.Smg. *Enrico Tazzoli,* being launched at Genoa on 14 October 1935.

Source: www.regiamarina.net

As Christiano d'Adamo of Regiamarina.net writes:

"Typical of this class was an increased range and an improved habitability, thus making the vessels very suitable for long cruises. Unfortunately, these units, slow in maneuvring, were better suited for isolated attacks against slow merchant ships than for group actions. Overall, they should be considered successful since the *Calvi* sunk 29,603 tons, the *Finzi* 26,222 and the *Tazzoli* 96,553."

The dimensions of these three submarines were 276.57 feet in the overall length, 25.3 feet wide, and 17.06 feet deep. Their displacement tonnage was 1,550 tons on the surface and 2,060 tons when submerged. They were propelled by twin 4,400 horsepower diesel engines that were backed up by a 1,800 horsepower secondary motor. These turned two propeller shafts and provided the vessel with 17.1 knots of speed on the surface and eight knots when submerged.

D'Adamo continues, "The standard propulsion system consisted of diesel engines for surface navigation and electric motors for submerged one. The *Ammiragli* and *Balilla* class had a third diesel engine attached to a Dynamo used to produce electricity for surface navigation, thus providing for low-speedlong-range capabilities." He notes that Italian submarines never fully researched or installed the Dutch-designed schnorchel device, which enabled the submarines to recharge their batteries and motor under diesel power while submerged.

The range of a *Calvi* class submarine was 11,400 nautical miles at eight knots on the surface, and was based on a carrying capacity of an impressive 75 tons of diesel. The primary armament consisted of eight torpedoes, each of 533 millimeter, fired from both fore and aft, as well as two 120 by 45-milimetre canons, located just forward and aft of the conning tower. There were an additional four anti-aircraft guns mounted on deck, each of 13.2 millimetres.

CARLO FECIA DI COSSATO & R.SMG. ENRICO TAZZOLI

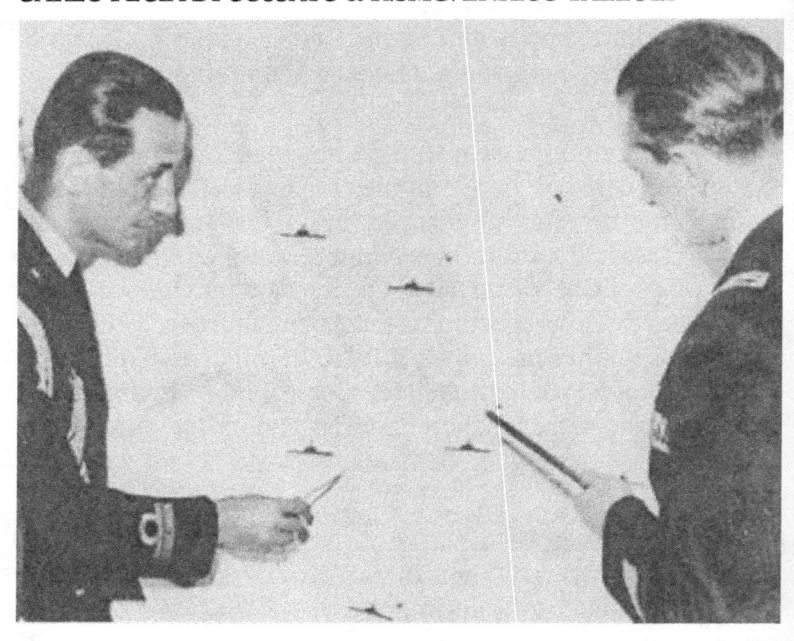

The caption for this photo from an Italian naval periodical reads: "Betasom officers discussing the modalities for the attack on the western Atlantic," and names Caridi (out of picture), Anfossi, and Polacchini (right). The chart is very interesting as it shows the Italian and German intent to penetrate the Caribbean, cut off the Windward Passage, place a boat at the mouth of the Northeast Providence Channel, and attack Florida. Per the chart below, they achieved most of these objectives, barring an attack on Florida that was forestalled by damage to the *Tazzoli* and never resumed. Later on, the Caribbean was also entered from the east.

Source: Francesco Mattesini, "The Attack of the Betasom Submarines from the Bahama Islands to the Coast of Venezuela (February-March, 1942)," from *The Bulletin*, the Archive of Naval History, Rome, 2014.

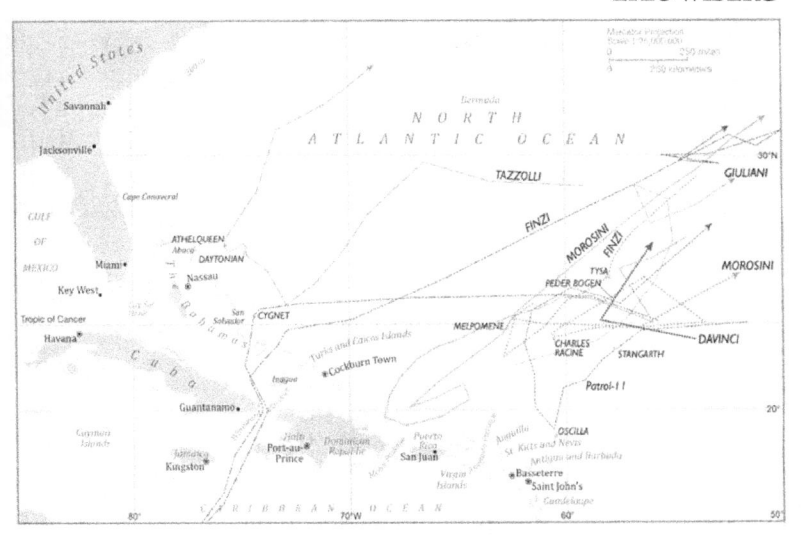

One of the unusual features of the submarine was that it was capable of carrying 72 men, versus the 48 to 55 required for a typical German Type VII or Type IX submarine. On her long patrol to the Bahamas, the *Tazzoli* would carry a complement of 60 men. The crew breakdown was typically seven officers and 65 crew-members. Since one of the most outcome-determinative persons on the submarine was the commander, it will be worth devoting several paragraphs to Carlo Fecia di Cossato, one of the most successful submarine commanders both in the Bahamas region and worldwide during World War II.

Di Cossato was born in Rome on the 25th of September 1908 to Carlo and Maria Luisa Gene. His belonged to a noble Piedmont family and he was invested with the title of Earl, part of the Savoy dynasty. He attended the Royal College at

Moncalieri, run by the Barnabiti brothers. Naval service ran in di Cossato's family: his father had lost an eye on the China station and his brother Luigi had received the silver medal for bravery for leadership during landings in Bargal, Somalia in 1925. Because Luigi had died during other exercises in Calabria, Carlo was denied his request to serve as an aircraft observer.

Carlo Fecia di Cossato, commander of the *Tazzoli* on its Bahamas patrol.

Source: piombino-storia.blogspot.com/2010/09/capitano-carlo-fecia-di-cossato.html

In 1923, he completed the equivalent of high school and entered the Naval Academy in Leghorn, graduating in 1928 with the rank first of Midshipman and then of Acting Sub-Lieutenant at the age of 19. His early assignments were aboard the submarine *Bausan*, a cruiser named *Ancona*, and a destroyer named *Nicotera*. After further classes he was assigned to the cruiser *Libia* in China, where he led amphibious troops in Shanghai. In 1933 the *Libia* returned to Italy and di Cossato participated in the defence of Massawa, in the Italian colony of Abyssinia.

After a brief staff assignment under Admiral De Feo in East Africa, di Cossato's next assignments were all in Libya on the torpedo boat *San Martino, Pollux* and *Alcione*. During the Spanish Civil War he served on submarines, taking part in two special missions to the coast of Iberia. In 1939he enrolled in submarine school. He became a Lieutenant aboard the submarine *Menotti* of the 34th Squadron in Messina. Then in the fall of 1940 he was transferred to Bordeaux to join the Betasom flotilla, the joint venture between the Regia Marina and the German *Kriegsmarine*, a portmanteau of for *Beta* for the B in Bordeaux and *Som* for *Sommergibili*, the Italian word for submarine.

Di Cossato served as second in command to Victor Raccanelli on the *Tazzoli*. Together they sank the Yugoslav steamer *Orao* off Scotland, and the British *Ardanhan* on 14 January. Then in early 1941 he was promoted from *Tenente di Vascello* (Lieutenant), to*Capitano di Corvetta* (Lieutenant Commander). The next promotion, all going well, would be *Capitano di Fregata* (Commander). On 5 April 1941 Raccanelli was removed from command and di Cossato was promoted and given his own command. After vigorous testing, the boat began its first patrol just two days later. A week later they found and sank the British ship *Aurillac*. The Norwegian ships *Fernlane* and *Alfred Olsen* followed. Di Cossato was establishing a level of success for himself in submarines.

On July 15th 1941 di Cossato and crew began another cruise from Bordeaux, this time to Freetown, Sierra Leone, West Africa. He attacked a convoy on 10th August without success. On the 12th, di Cossato was given unconfirmed credit for damaging a ship called either the *Sangar*a or *Zangara* of

British registry. On the 19th of August he sank the Norwegian tanker *Sildra*. In August of 1940 the *Tazzoli* and her men were re-assigned to Bordeaux, France as part of the Betasom flotilla. On November 22nd 1941 the British cruisers HMS *Devonshire* and HMS *Dorsetshire* used Allied Enigma code-breaking to intercept and sink two of the most active German raiders of either world war: the *Atlantis* under Bernard Rogge, and the *Python*, in the southern Central Atlantic. Then they fled the scene, leaving over 414 men in need of rescue. As a result Admiral Dönitz activated all the larger Italian submarines they could spare, reducing their manning to a minimum to make room for the passengers. In an extraordinary rescue, *Tazolli* and other Italian and German submarines managed to load 254 men on their deck casings, and in a slow convoy proceeded back to Saint Nazaire in time for Christmas.

A rare contemplative wartime photo, showing di Cossato reading during a patrol in the multi-windowed, dry and wind-proof bridge of the *Tazzoli* in the Atlantic. By contrast, the conning towers of German U-boats were completely exposed.

Source: Marcello Marpola betasom.it/forum index.php?showtopic=28909&page=1

On a macro level, d'Adamo writes that Dönitz, "attempted to integrate the Italian forces in the wolf-pack strategy, but the Italian boats were technically poor, slow to dive, and possessed a large and easily detectable profile. As a result, most Italian submarines operated in the Central and Southern Atlantic in solitary missions." Indeed it is precisely these kinds of missions which the *Finzi, Tazzoli, Morosini, Leonardo da Vinci*, and *Calvi* undertook to the Bahamas area lone wolves self-supported in the operational area above all else by each other in the transfer of fuel and torpedoes.

The caption for this photo is "1942 - CC Fecia di Cossato, commander of R. Smg. *Tazzoli*, and T.V. Gazzana Priaroggia, second in command on deck, at a meeting in the Atlantic with another Italian submarine." This was almost certainly taken in the Bahamas area where the Betasom boats operated free from Allied air attack. The other submarine is probably the *Finzi* or *Morosini*.

Source: Marcello Marpola betasom.it/forum/index. Php?showtopic=28909&page=1

CARLO FECIA DI COSSATO & R.SMG. ENRICO TAZZOLI

Tazzoli began its Bahamas patrol on the 2nd of February 1942, sailing from Bordeaux. Her assigned area was to the east of Florida and the Bahamas. However, because she would be so busy sinking ships she would never have the fuel to approach Florida or enter the Caribbean to the Yucatan Channel. *Tazzoli* was the first Italian sub sent to the region, but not the first to arrive, as the *Finzi* preceded her. On the way out she encountered and fired three torpedoes at the British tanker *Rapana* in daylight on March 3rd. Due to interference ofthesea conditions, all missed, and the boat continued westwards.

Three days later, on March 6th, the *Tazzoli* came upon the Dutch steamer *Astrea* and sank her. The following day the *Tazzoli* destroyed the Norwegian tanker *Tonsbergsfjord*.

War trophy: the crew of the *Tazzoli* display a life ring from the Norwegian merchant ship *Tonsbergsfjord*. Note the large portals, which German U-boats did not have, and the head of an Italian sailor peering through one of them upper right.

Source: Antonio Maronari, "*Un Sommergibile non e Rientrato Alla Base.*"

The 32 surviving Norwegians later met survivors of the *Montevideo*, also sunk by the *Tazzoli*, in lifeboats on the high seas, and were rescued by the same ship (the *Telamon*). Together they reached Haiti (they were mistaken for Germans when they landed in lifeboats) and then Curacao. Sunk on the 8th of March, the *Montevideo* was a steam ship from Uruguay that had ironically been built in Italy as the *Adamello* in 1920 and commandeered by the Uruguayans. Claims that the neutral ship was sunk by Germans inflamed anti-German nationalism in Uruguay, leading to protests and eventual abandonment of its neutrality, which had crucially allowed the German cruiser *Graf Spee* to seek refuge there after the Battle of the River Plate earlier in the war.

At that point in the patrol the *Tazzoli* was expected to enter the Caribbean Sea (which the sister submarine *Finzi* ultimately achieved, going as far as between Aruba and Jamaica without sinking anything), and proceed to the Yucatan Peninsula at the underbelly of the United States and the Gulf of Mexico. The Italian naval historian Francesco Mattesini relates that di Cossato was in radio contact with Betasom headquarters up to the 10th of March, and it was agreed that the *Tazzoli* no longer had sufficient fuel to enable it to reach Yucatan and return.

Instead di Cossato "decided to remain among the Bahama Islands and the island of Bermuda, where the current traffic seemed very favourable. He requested authorization and informed base that he had already sunk three ships in that area. At the same time, considering he had just nine torpedoes, he asked Betasom to receive more torpedoes from the *Finzi*. The request was, however, rejected," in part because the damaged *Finzi* had been ordered to refuel the *Morosini* instead. This set up the *Tazzoli* for a fateful and destructive cruise to the Bahamas instead off to the Caribbean.

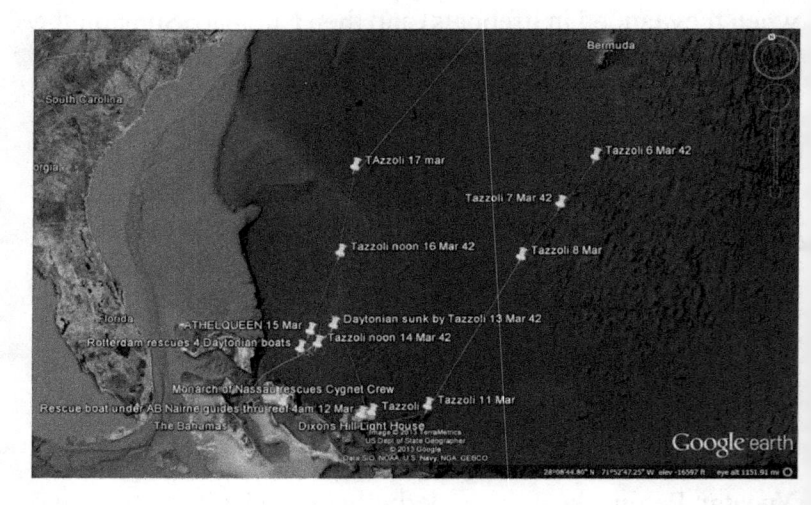

R.Smg. *Enrico Tazzoli*'s patrol through the Bahamas and Bermuda regions, 6 to 17 March, 1942, showing three ships struck in Bahamas.

Source: Google Earth, data by author with input from Platon Alexiades.

Chapter 2

S.S.*CYGNET,* HISTORY, OWNERS & CHARTERERS

The *Cygnet* was ordered on the December 1st 1915 and built as the steam ship *Mirach* in 1917 by the Rotterdam Dry Dock Company of the Netherlands. She was launched on the March 3rd 1917, completed as yard number 61, and delivered on the June 6th that year. Her original owners were the N.V. Van Nievelt, Goudriaan & Company's Steamship Company, also known as Nigoco. For the next year the *Mirach*'s flag was Dutch, and her home-port was Rotterdam. Then on March 21st 1918, with the rush of World War I still on, the United States government (the Emergency Fleet Corporation, managed by the United States Shipping Board) purchased the ship and registered it to New York. Somehow, although not configured with passenger accommodation, the *Mirach* managed to bring 31 emigrants to Ellis Island from Rotterdam on the 6th of July 1917, 46 from Bordeaux France on the July 23rd 1918, and 31 more on the January 1st 1926.

S.S. CYGNET, HISTORY, OWNERS, & CHARTERERS

The ship's American ownership only lasted for a year, and then in 1919 it reverted to Nigoco in Rotterdam, where she continued to trade under her original name for the next 20 years, until 1939. *Mirach* joined Nigoco's Rotterdam-South American Line, visiting such ports as Antwerp, Rotterdam, Leixoes (Portugal), Lisbon, Rio de Janeiro, Santos, Santa Fé, Rosario, Paranagua, Victoria, Bahia (Brazil), Rotterdam, and Antwerp. On March 11th 1927, she received a new radio callsign whilst in Rotterdam.

The *Mirach*'s gross tonnage was 3,530 and her overall length 361'4". She is described as a general cargo ship, fabricated of steel, with a single flush deck. There were no accommodations for passengers. The ship's beam was 49'8" and the draft was 21'7." Her cargo carrying capacity was 6,367 tons, or 336,000 cubic feet of grain or bales. By 1942 her 1,500 horsepower, three-cylinder, triple-expansion steam engine propelled *Cygnet* at an average speed of between 9 and 9.5 knots utilizing a single propeller.

On May 27th 1939, roughly three months prior to the outbreak of World War II, *Mirach* was sold to the Goulandris Brothers of Andros & Piraeus, Greece and London, who renamed her *Cygne*t and flagged and registered her to Panama. The name originates from *cycnus*, Latin for young swan, or *kýknos* in Greek.

Cycnus, for young swan, or *kýknos* in Greek. Photographed in the stream flowing from Stenies, Andros. Locals boaters told the author that on calm days they encounter the swans out to sea.

Source: Author's photo, 2016.

A wartime entry for another Goulandris-owned ship operating in the Americas (the *Ioannis Goulandris*), listed the owners as Greek Line (line for operators/brand), Greek Royal Government (owners), and Greek Line, 8-10 Bridge Street, New York City, as local agents. Ascertaining precise ship ownership can be a global and confusing sport.

According to Greek academics, the Goulandris "…family's investments in steamships began with Ioannis P. Goulandris (18401928), while in the 1920s the second generation of his five sons (Peter, Michael, Basil, Nicholas, and Leonidas) founded the company Goulandris Bros, which grew during the interwar years into the second most powerful ship-owning group after the Kulukundis family. On the eve of the Second World War, Goulandris Bros was managing a fleet of 20 steamships. The third generation of the family, which split into four different groups, established the Goulandris' at the pinnacle of Greek ship owning for at least the first three

post-war decades." (Harlaftis and Theotokas, "*Leadership in World Shipping Greek Family Firms in International Business*," Palgrave MacMillan, UK, 2009). By the end of World War II, New York City had become a new centre for the family investments.
\

In 1939, the firm had moved from Chora, Andros, to Megaron Laikis, Navarino Street, in Piraeus port near Athens. In London, their offices were then at 59 Saint Mary Axe. With the fall of Greece to Italy and the Germans, the headquarters were moved to London, with an office at 8-10 Bridge Street, New York behind the huge Customs House at the very southern tip of Manhattan. The firm's subsidiaries included the Halcyon Steamship Company, also known as the Greek Steamship Line. Nicholas, Leonidas, and Basil Goulandris, who also operated Goulandris Brothers, owned the Greek Line. Not uncharacteristically for shipping firms globally, there was yet another subsidiary at the same addresses, known as the General Steam Ship Navigation Company of Greece, owned by Basil J., Nicolas J., and Leonidas J. Goulandris. A US legal case based on a 1940 voyage may clarify the relationships:

"Goulandris Brothers (Hellas) Ltd. is a corporation organized and existing under the laws of the Kingdom of Greece which acted as agents and managers in Greece for vessels owned by the three Goulandris brothers and other persons. The firm managed the vessel on the voyage in suit, on behalf of, and with the authority of, the owners. ...General Steam Navigation Co. Ltd. of Greece ("Greek Line") is a corporation organized and incorporated in Piraeus, in July 1939. Greek Line acted as agent for the owners of the vessel for the collection of freight." In other words the three brothers owned the ship (90% of it) and the Greek Line operated it: "Basil, Leonidas and Nicholas Goulandris, were brothers, residents of Greece and, at the times relevant, each owned a 30% interest, respectively, in the S.S. *Ioannis P. Goulandris*. A 10% interest in various shares in the vessel was owned by a number of other persons."

TradeWinds, a leading shipping industry journal, relates that "When talk turns to the island of Andros, the names that spring to mind will certainly include Goulandris and Embiricos. These are two of the families dating back several generations whose names emblazon streets and squares in Andros town, also known as Chora..... Stenies [is] referred to as 'the sea captains' village."

One of the patriarchs of the shipping family, Vasilis (Basil) P. Goulandris was born in Andros, in 1913. His twin brother was Nicholas, and his other brothers were John, George, and Constantine. His obituary in 1994 notes that Andros traces "a rich heritage in merchant shipping for at least three centuries. Goulandris was descended from a long line of individuals who, for at least three prior generations, in varying capacities, made their living from merchant shipping. Some were captains, others were chief engineers, and eventually more than a few of them and their descendants became shipowners themselves." His long-time wife was Elisa Karadontis, described as an 'Athenian beauty.'

Another obituary points out, "The family had owned sailing ships in the last century which they operated in the Mediterranean and in the Black Sea routes. They were also

S.S. CYGNET, HISTORY, OWNERS, & CHARTERERS

among the first Greek ship-owners to acquire steamships before the turn of this century. As Basil was entering his teens, discussions around the family table - or on the bridges of family motor-ships - centred around the comparative advantages of steel vessels and the economies afforded by the latest British-made coal-fired boiler."

The Goulandris Brothers' house flag, or company identifier, is described by one expert (Jordan in his "Merchant Fleets 1939"), as "Black with blue gamma (Greek G) on white band, bordered by two narrow blue bands or yellow with black top, separated by blue band bearing white gamma." The hull was black with a red boot-stripe between hull and waterline. The ships were engaged in "general tramping," indicating that no fixed routes or "lines" were undertaken, rather cargos of opportunity were chased after globally on a spot, or opportunistic basis.

Source: http://www.crwflags.com/fotw/flags/gr~hfgou.html, Jordan, page 208

According to an original charter party for the *Cygnet* kept on file at their offices in London, Goulandris Bros served as managers for the Halcyon Steamship Company Limited of Piraeus. The *Halcyon* was a Dutch-built sister ship to the *Cygnet*, which met its end in the western Atlantic, a victim of U-109 northeast of Bermuda on February 6th 1942. The standard time charter agreement gave *Cygnet*'s coal consumption as 22 tons "of best Welsh coal" a day, to be shovelled into the steam engine by hard-working men called stokers and trimmers. The charterers were Ocean Dominion Steamship Corporation of New York. The contract gave them the option of loading in La Guaira, Venezuela, Georgetown, British Guiana, and/or Trinidad, Barbados, or the Dominican Republic, even including the West Indies. The discharge range was from St. Lawrence and/or Saguenay, Canada, but not above 50 degrees north latitude.

Maritime enthusiast Neale Rosanoski writes that Ocean Dominion provided "one of the services operated by the Aluminium Company of America for the bauxite trade from British Guiana to Canada from the 1920s. In 1940 it, together with the fellow companies Aluminium Line and the American Caribbean Line were consolidated into Alcoa Steamship Co." In August 1940 the *Cygnet* was delivered to Ocean Dominion in La Guairia, after she had cleared outward bound. Charterers were to pay extra insurance not to exceed US$1,500, and the agreed price per ton of bunker coal was $6 per ton. The rate of hire was $3 per ton of the ship's total carrying capacity, which was listed as 6,391 tons, for rough charter hire of $19,173 per month, or $230,076 a year roughly two thirds of the ship's value.

The agreement provided charterers with the latitude of about 10 days to declare a re-delivery date or port, however it is explicitly added that "No deck cargo to be shipped," although in fact her final cargo included bales of rubber on deck. Victualing, or food for officers and crew, was to be maintained at the current rate, rather than a stipulated daily amount. The shipbrokers were Simpson, Spence & Young of London, New York, and Glasgow - interestingly Wallis

Simpson's second father-in-lawfounded the firm.(As the Duchess of Windsor, she would lead the Bahamas Red Cross in the colony over which her husband, the Duke of Windsor, was governor between 1940 and 1945).

Along with the standard verbiage on the one-page document is an Amended Jason Clause which reads, "In the event of accident, danger, damage, or disaster.... resulting from any cause whatsoever.... [where] the shipowner is not responsible by statute or contract or otherwise, the shippers, consignees, or owners of the cargo shall contribute with the shipowner in general average to the payment of any securities, losses or expenses....".The Carriage of Goods by Sea Act, or COGSA, a US law enacted in 1936, covered the voyage. Presciently, the Baltime War Risk Clause of 1920 (named after the Baltic Exchange in London and time, versus "spot" charter) applied. It read in part, "In case of war, the following special provisions to apply: Steamer not to be sent on any voyage before Owners have been able to cover her full value against war risk. Charterers to refund Owners any war premium, and if same is not paid promptly on production of receipt, same to be considered as non-payment of hire."

"No passengers to be carried, unless Charterers procure guarantees satisfactory to Owners, that the passengers do not expose vessel to the risk of being sunk or captured or to any other war risk. Excluding passengers, mahogany, explosives, dangerous and injurious cargo, arms, ammunition, acids, and regular ore trade but understood privilege loading bauxite. Charterers paying war risk on Owner's valuation of $360,000, at Owner's option, Owners effecting war risk insurance and Charterers refunding same immediately, but understood not exceeding one-half percent."

That agreement was in 1940. On April 28th 1941, 34-year-oldSecond Engineer ConstantinosSofos signed aboard in Philadelphia. In his diary written in April 1942 he shared insights into the *Cygnet*'s trading patterns before the US and Canada were attacked by German and Italian submarines:"I was recruited on s/s *Cygnet*of the Greek Lines. On May 1st we sailed for Sydney, [Nova Scotia], where we delivered the ship to Dominion Shipping Co. Ltd., a charter company. We stayed there making trips to and from Wabana, atransporting minerals [red hematire, or iron ore] to Sydney. Though those trips were safe from the dangers of war [until 1943, when four ships were sunk there], they were extremely tedious. The duration of each trip was 40 sailing hours and 15 hours in each port for loading and unloading."Situated northwest of St. John's, Wabana stands for "place where the light shines first" in the Beothuk tongue.

Panamanian-flagged, Greek-owned, Dutch-built *Cygnet*, under her former name *Mirach*between 1939 and 1940, during the war, but before she was flagged to Panama.

Source: wrecksite.eu/wreck.aspx?194990

S.S. CYGNET, HISTORY, OWNERS, & CHARTERERS

An image of the Goulandris Bros' fleet's house colours on one of their ship's stacks. The *Cygnet* was still painted with this logo when sunk, as confirmed by a film of her demise captured by the Italians. Owners confirmed this to the author whilst watching the film together in London in 2015.

Source: Aleksi Lindström, shipspotting.com/gallery/Photo.php?lid=1371933

Chapter 3

CYGNET'S OFFICERS & MEN

The Greek Captain, John Mamais (it is possible his birth name is Ioannis, Jannis, or Iannis), led the crew of 30 on *Cygnet's* final voyage. Twenty-seven of the men on board were Greek, with one citizen each from Canada, Romania, and Spain. Many of them Captain Mamais, Chief Officer Antonios Falangas, Second Officer John Aeginitis, Chief Engineer Dimitrios Vlachakis, and Greaser Antonios Xanthos were from Andros, the same seafaring island from which the owning Goulandris family hailed.

The view from behind the Falangas house in Stenies toward Chora, situated in the next valley, on Andros, in the Cyclades Islands of Greece.

Source: Author photo, with thanks to Capt. Makis and Mrs. Eleni Kourtesis.

The fact that the three most senior deck and the engineering officers were all from Andros suggests that the owners trusted sailors from that locale to run their ships well. Also, it isnot surprising given that ship owners from the eastern island of Chios can claim to control 40% of Greek shipping; Chians are also well represented. Wireless Operator George Lemos (from a family with deep ship owning roots), Donkeyman Demetreos Koukoulis, firemen (the labourers who stoked the coal holds) Marinos Tsilimas and Michael Katradis, and coal trimmers Michael Brillis and Stilianos Kalogeras were all from Chios.

The Greek sailors hailed from many islands and ports in that nation: Tilos, Nisyros, Amorgos, Hydra, Corfu, Cephalonia, Kavalla, Lemonia, Crete, Syra, Piraeus, and Lavrila. Those were the ports they were born by 1942 most of them listed Piraeus, Athens, or Andros as their permanent homes, though it was by that time under German occupation. Their *de facto* bases were the offices of the owners, and the union hiring halls of New York.

Deck Boy Pio Arrizubieta, aged 29, hailed from Orihuela, Spain and was based in neutral Bilbao. The hometown of the 24-year-old Messman George Morrison (no doubt an adopted name) was Gudutal Arad Comuma Socador, on the Romanian border with Hungary. According to meticulous immigration records, the 30 men ranged in height from 5'2" (three men) to 5'11" (Falangas and Paulos Tsiridanakis); most had brown eyes, but several had blue, hazel, or grey orbs; most were fair complexioned and had brown hair; and none had scars or tattoos, at least so far as the inspectors could determine.

Captain Mamais was 5'6" and weighed 150 pounds. He was born on Andros in 1904, and his wife, Kula, was living in Piraeus at the time. Antonios, or Anthony Falangas, was the son and father of Stratis Falangas. The name is said to originate from the trees placed beneath new boats to enable them to roll into the ocean, and was used to describe shipwrights. He was born in the village of Stenies, Andros, which is in the next valley over from Chora, where owners dwelt.

The Falangas house in Stenies, the "Captain's village," of Andros, Greece, in 2016.

Source: Author photo, 2016.

The son of Eustratios Falangas, they moved to 15 Theofiles, Athens as a young man, and he rose in the merchant shipping industry to become first officer, or second in command of the *Cygnet*, essentially above everyone except fellow Androsians Captain Mamais and Chief Engineer Vlachakis. Born on October 3rd, 1911, Falangas was 5'11" and 185 pounds. He had a cut across the centre of his right temple, possibly caused by the subsequent *Cygnet* attack. In 1941 he and other mariners were staying at ¼ Bury Street, London, waiting to ship out.

Second officer, Ioannis S. (John) Eginitis, he was 5'8" inches tall and 175 pounds. William Forest Dods was born in Scotland on September 14th 1912, and was 30 when he served as third officer of the *Cygnet* in 1942. In 1926, at age 14, he sailed from Southampton for New York as a student aboard the Royal Mail steamer *Orduna*. Ironically he stayed at the Imperial Hotel in London (he would later stay in a hotel of the same name in Nassau). Dods stood 5'7" tall, weighed 178 pounds and had dark brown hair and green eyes. He became a naturalized Canadian citizen. In August 1937 Dods returned from New York to London, this time aboard the *Queen Mary*. By 1942 his hometown was Sudbury, Ontario.

Constantinos (Gus) Sofos, aged 34, the second assistant engineer of the *Cygnet*.

Source: His son, Nicholas (Nick) Sofos of Connecticut.

Constantinos Sofos' tale of joining the *Cygnet* is wrought with personal and professional obstacles. However, this may have been demonstrative of the experiences of many Allied sailors looking for stable work in tumultuous times, when home countries became off limits, and sailors were cut off from families as well as news of their fates. Writing immediately after his service on the *Cygnet*, Sofos relates that: "I departed from Greece on March 2nd 1940, and arrived in London on March 7th. I remained there awaiting the SS *Mount Kassion* until March 28, when I left for Liverpool, where I joined the crew of said steamer."

"We sailed with this steamship between England and Canadian ports. However, due to a certain dramatic adventure, I was laid off on July 22, 1940. During the period of my stay in Liverpool I became witness to countless air raids and spent several nights in bomb shelters. Caught in such a predicament, I considered it prudent to go to America, and on October 27th 1940, I was recruited on *Mount Othrys*. On October 28th 1940, the day Italy declared war on Greece, I sailed from Liverpool for Baltimore. I stayed about 15 days and then I was dismissed (laid off) from the steamship. On the December 5^{th}1940,I left for New York, determined to find some kind of work and stay until the end of the war. However, unfortunately, despite all my efforts, it proved impossible. I experienced at that time the most miserable days in my life. Being a merchant mariner, I could legally stay and rest up to 2 months before being recruited for another voyage, but I had already exceeded that limit and I was liable to prosecution."

"Being in a dire financial situation," he continued, "and having lost every hope of finding work to sustain myself, I was forced to leave on April 28th 1941, for Philadelphia, where I was recruited on SS *Cygnet*." As history played out, the concerted Axis invasion of Greece began that very month, with the country being occupied thereafter by Germans, Italians, and Bulgarians.

Sailor Gerasimos Antzoulatos of Cephalonia in 1940 at the age of 19. He emigrated to the US after the *Cygnet*'s unexpected demise near Florida.

Source: His son Nikos Antzoulatos, 2017.

Chapter 4

CYGNET'S FINAL VOYAGE, FEB. 10ᵗʰ MAR. 11ᵗʰ, 1942

Cygnet's charterers for her final voyage from Canada to South America and back to Portland Maine were Saguenay Terminals Company of Montreal, which was part of the Aluminium Company of Canada. According to historian Ian Coombe, "Sagterms **operated under the two main branches. The sphere of the Demerara-Saguenay Division, in Montreal, was transportation. This included transportation of raw materials and finished products for the parent company, the Aluminium Company of Canada, as well as general cargo.**"

Despite the firm losing four bulk ships to German U-boats early in the war, "**By the 1940's the U.S. War Shipping Administration was allocating vessels to Sagterms, and by 1942 over 100 had been either allocated or chartered to carry company cargo.** In 1939 Sagterms began with three vessels sailing an ocean lane that connected the majestic rock-walled Saguenay [River] in Quebec with the exotic jungle-lined Demerara in British Guiana."

Sofos relates that "around the end of December [1941] we sailed from Sydney [NS] for Halifax where the charter company was to deliver the boat to the owners and then we would take it to New York for repairs. However, because of a dispute among the owners, the charterers and insurance, we remained there until February 10th 1942, when we left [Halifax] for British Guiana. With the aid of directives from the Department of Navy Control, and sailing in great distress, we miraculously escaped the submarines and arrived at Georgetown, British Guiana on February 22."

Because of the shallow draft at the mouth of the Demerara River, *Cygnet* had to leave Guiana with space in the cargo holds, intending to top up on cargo at another port. Sofos confirms, "after receiving a part of the mineral cargo [ore], because the draught didn't allow loading the entire cargo, we left on February 28th for Saint Thomas [Virgin Islands], West Indies, where we docked on March 7th 1942. After we loaded the rest of the cargo, we departed for Portland, Maine." It was the night of March 7th to 8th 25 years almost to the day since the ship had been launched in the Netherlands.

Routing instructions were issued by the British authorities in British Guiana and by the Americans in Saint Thomas. They called for the ship to follow the coast as closely as practical. Based on those instructions, the *Cygnet* would have gained the open Atlantic through the Anegada or Mona

Passage, then passed north of the Turks and Caicos, hugging the shores in those days of celestial navigation and dead reckoning lurching from the comforting reassurance of one lighthouse to another, until they reached the coast of the American mainland.

Chapter 5

ATTACK, MARCH 11th, 1942

The voyage proceeded uneventfully for three days until the late afternoon of Wednesday, the 11th of March 1942. Radio Operator George Lemos, 29, was sitting in the radio shack. There was a lookout on the deck, and three lookouts on the bridge: Captain Mamais, age 37, Chief Officer Falangas, 31, and a helmsman. The weather was clear, the sea slight, and visibility good. The ship was headed north, unarmed and not zig zagging. Since it was a bright sunny afternoon, they were not using any lights. Since no ships were known to have been sunk in the region, their guard was down.

ATTACK, MARCH 11TH, 1942

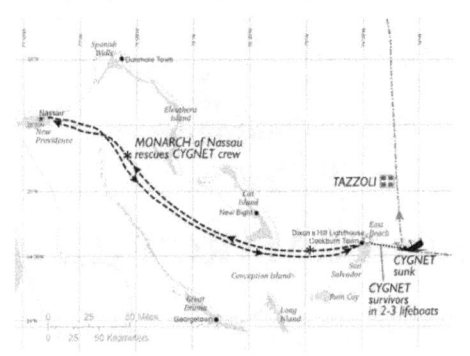

At 4:48 pm local time Falangas saw a torpedo emerge from beneath the ship on the port side, quite deep, heading towards land at a right angle to the bridge, which it appeared to have barely missed. At that point the ship's officers were using the lighthouse at Dixon Hill, on San Salvador, as a navigational reference. They were less than six miles away from the light, which was bearing 305 degrees. The *Cygnet* was steering almost due north - 350 degrees - and was making roughly nine knots.

The lighthouse at Dixon Hill, north-eastern San Salvador Island, Bahamas. Built on John Dixon's land in 1887, it is 163' tall, visible 19 miles, and its 400,000 candle power light is still wound by hand every 2.25 hours, making it very rare.

Source: homeaway.com/vacation-rental/p161215

Falangas immediately called Captain Mamais over to see the torpedo's wake. Suddenly there was an explosion forward, by the Number One hatch. Chief Engineer Vlachakis, 34, happened to be on deck at the time of the impact. He saw the torpedo approaching. When it hit, he saw the heavy cargo hatch being blown off and "a cloud of dust and debris rise several hundred feet with the explosion." He ran aft to the engine room and stopped the engine according to Sofos he did this using a jury-rigged lever on deck designed for just a contingency. From the bridge Mamais and Falangas watched in horror as the donkey engine, a steam contraption for enabling men to do heavy lifting such as raising and lowering the gangways, was shattered into little bits by the explosion.

Sofos continued: "Our journey was smooth for about four days, and we were already near the Bahamas, across from Florida, when our ship was hit by a torpedo at the #1 hold. It was 4:50 pm. The hatches were blown up, small and large pieces of debris covered the deck, and the ship started listing immediately at the bow. Although it was my shift, at that moment I happened to be at the stern inspecting the rudder. In the engine room was my assistant, a greaser. For the auto-breaking of the engine and the circulation pump, which was operating independently form the engine, I had installed a system of my own patent that enabled me to control the engine from the deck, thus the engine was easily put on idle. There was slight confusion during the lowering of the starboard life boat, but although the torpedo hit the vessel at a critical spot, luckily, the entire crew of 30 men boarded the 2 lifeboats without a single loss of life."

ATTACK, MARCH 11TH, 1942

Antonio Maronari, a member of the Italian crew, recorded events from the attacker's point of view: "We are en route to the Bahamas... Land ahoy! Shouts [signalman] Guerrini Passon at [1:30 pm local time]. Distant and blurred, there lies the island of San Salvador... Rather than proceeding immediately to the Crooked Island Passage (between that harmonious island and Long Island in the Bahamas group), as previously agreed, the commander decides to stay here for a few days to make the most of this excellent area." Mattesini notes that only half an hour passed between when the *Tazzoli* first sighted the Bahamas and their first target loomed over the horizon from the south. Maronari records that they waited 1.5 hours between seeing San Salvador and overhearing George Lemos on the *Cygnet*'s radio. He wrote that Radio Petty Officer Domenico Botta "intercepted the transmission of a nearby ship, followed by another, in which a coastal radio station signals to the American steamers that an enemy submarine is in the Caribbean Sea. The *Tazzoli* perhaps? We are six miles offshore of San Salvador... It's [3 pm]. The gunner [Midshipman Giuseppi Centelli], whilst on the lookout at starboard, has spotted a ship. We accelerate at full speed and perform a fast manoeuvre [at 4 pm] in order to attack under water. The commander has taken position at the attack periscope... besides him; the chief torpedo-man is ready to press the 5th and 6th switch of the [torpedo] launch device...

5 out! 6 out! It is [4:45 pm]....

It has barely been a minute.

"Hit! Surface...!" shouts the Corsair of the Atlantic [di Cossato] as a tremendous roar rumbles into the abyss." Mattesini's account is in accord, with him noting that di Cossato dove and began lining the sub up for an attack as soon as the ship was sighted. He states that the Italian commander fired two stern torpedoes, and that they struck after 30 seconds. We know that the first passed harmlessly beneath the ship and continued onwards towards San Salvador.

Aboard the *Cygnet*, the torpedo struck forward, about eight feet below the water line. So large was the hole that according to Vlachakis, water was up to the well decks before the lifeboats could even be lowered. Immediately, the ship took on an angle of sinking by the bow, or head. She also drifted to starboard, but did not list heavily to that side. Fortunately none of the crew was badly injured, and all of them proceeded in an orderly fashion to launch the lifeboats. Photos of the ship show large boats on either side, plus at least one jolly boat, or harbour launch, on the bridge deck on the port side. Of these, two lifeboats were used that afternoon.

Lemos was able to get an SSS (submarine sighted surfaced) signal off by radio, but he was unaware of their exact position, so he ran from the radio shack to the bridge to jot it down. However, the officers were already abandoning ship. He saw the men in the boats beckoning him to join and he did so. Although Lemos was thus unable to give shore stations a position, Vlachakis wryly noted, "sent SOS but did not send position no time. Position sent from San Salvador Island (*they saw it*)." Indeed he was right, as residents on the nearby island, who were drawn to the beach by the sound of shells exploding, were witnessing the attack with great

ATTACK, MARCH 11ᵀᴴ, 1942

excitement. Mamais recorded that "the ship settled by the head and all officers and crew took to the life boats, and as soon as the life boats were lowered a submarine appeared and fired a blank shell to warn the life boats away from the ship."

Sofos observed, "as soon as we got a few meters away from the ship, we saw the submarine surfacing and a few moments later it was floating on the surface. We then noticed that 2 members of the crew were on the tower and were waiving their hands in salutation. While we were saluting back, we saw another 2 men from the crew running; one towards the bow deck gun, and the other towards the stern deck gun. They started firing at our ship, which seemed like a fearless giant refusing to yield to the enemy's gunshots. Meanwhile, from the moment the engine was set to idle, the steam boiler's safety valves began to whistle, as if the ship was sending us its farewell, which lasted until the ship sank, after the 7th, which was the last missile to hit it. The drama began at 4:50 pm, and it was concluded at 6:20 pm."

The *Tazzoli* surfaced about one mile off the starboard quarter, or right flank. They fired a warning shell to be sure that the boats stayed clear of the ship, which they fully intended to destroy. The boats pulled clear to a quarter to a half-mile astern. The diarist Maronari wrote: "We head towards the slightly heeled ship, the boats of the castaways already floating around it. In seconds, we are laying the guns. After a few minutes the boats are already far: we can open fire without fear of hitting them. A few castaways greet us, waving their arms. We return the salute in disbelief. Then, without worrying about the proximity of the land, from which they can easily see and follow all the action, we open up [fire] on the ship that is down by bow. Seven 120 [45-millimetre] rounds pierce the hull at the waterline. Amid the smoke, we distinguish the name of our fourth victim on the taffrail: *Cygnet* - Panama." Again Mattesini agrees, writing that "men sent to the fore cannon made seven shots, which reached the height of the ship's cargo line, or Plimsoll marks, which were exposed and visible. Di Cossato recognized that it was the elderly Panamanian freighter *Cygnet*." Captain Mamais observed, "...When the life boats were between a quarter and a half mile from the ship the submarine circled the ship and fired six shells into the ship." First the submariners sent shells hurling into the starboard side, then they rounded the stern and shelled the port side.

Maronari recorded, "the deck is sideways and the high smokestack vents steam: one of the rounds has landed on the bridge, operating the siren which is now emitting a whining sound. From afar, the castaways are motionlessly watching on... ...it may even seem that they are commenting on the accuracy and the effects of our fire. At this time the commander recalls an American radio program a few days back, in which the speaker said that: 'Never have the Italian submarines reached the shores of the United States.' The ship slowly sinks. We run at full speed towards the survivor in the boats and, as we approach, the lieutenant and the crew spontaneously shout 'good luck.' Commander Cossato waves the *Tricolore* flag in the air and shouts in English:

'Tell the Americans 'it isn't true. The Italian submarines have come here to sink their ships!' The castaways respond by energetically waving and shouting

ATTACK, MARCH 11ᵀᴴ, 1942

cheerfully. These exchanges are extraordinarily friendly, especially since in similar circumstances we could rather expect a series of mishaps."

The Greeks underestimated the number of shots fired, though Mamais was close, estimating that six missiles were used to sink his ship. Vlachakis described their firing as "leisurely." Others said they fired a shell about every minute. Asked whether the Italians communicated with their Greek victims, Vlachakis said that the "enemy merely waved." He said the *Tazzoli* looked old and rusty.

A live-action image of *Cygnet* being shelled by the *Tazzoli* smoke from guns at left, and exploding amidships. Taken by a member of the Italian naval crew.

Source: Readers can watch the video online for free at youtube.com/watch?v=aAnJBU4L9g4, starting 2:54 minutes:seconds.

SWAN SINKS

A rare and clear photo of *Cygnet* after the crew had abandoned ship, but while the engine is still emitting steam. Note the awning frame astern for the tropics. The whistle was shrieking at the time this photo was taken. The railing of the *Tazzoli* visible to the lower right indicates how close the sub got to the ship. Note relatively calm seas and good visibility. Taken from the starboard side of the sub as it round the ship's stern to port.

Source: Francesco Mattesini, *The Bulletin, The Archive of Military History*, 2014.

A rare still image from film, showing *Cygnet*'s stern with her name and that of Panama visible on the transom in the final moments before she plunged, abandoned, to the depths off San Salvador.

Source: Imperial War Museum, London, "Submarine surfaces after hitting ship. Small steamer is shelled and sunk." Item 3 of DW 633/44/42 of 21/10/1942.

ATTACK, MARCH 11TH, 1942

Clearly convinced that the ship was doomed, di Cossato motored off in a northerly direction at about 5:45 pm. They had been on the surface for roughly 50 minutes. According to some of the crew, the submarine submerged as it headed north. But, since Maronari wrote about seeing the boilers explode and the glow of the burning ship in the dusk, it would seem that di Cossato was rather unconcerned about a counter-attack, and he remained on the surface for some time. Captain Mamais wrote, "the life boats waited about an hour until the ship sank, and then pulled for the shore of San Salvador, or Watling Island…three or four of the crew having suffered minor injuries during the explosion." The *Cygnet* was observed to sink by her crew at 6:20 pm, an hour and a half after the initial attack.

A rare image of one of *Cygnet*'s lifeboats bobbing in the sea during the attack.

Source: youtube.com/watch?v=aAnJBU4L9g4

A final image of *Cygnet*, ablaze at the stern and very low in the water, by *Tazzoli*.

Source: youtube.com/watch?v=aAnJBU4L9g4

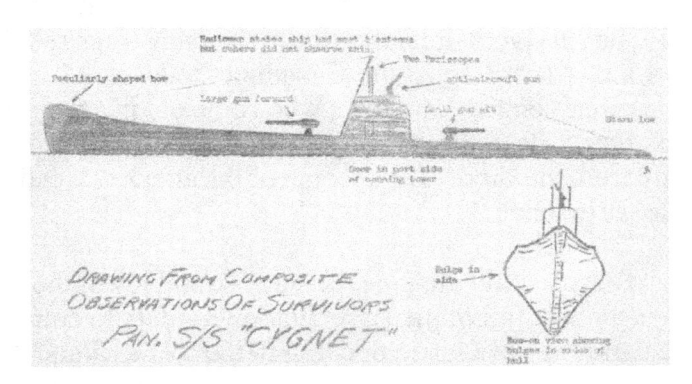

Drawing of *Tazzoli* as described to US Navy interrogators, Miami, March 21st.

Source: *Survivors Statements*, National Archives and Record Administration, USA

ATTACK, MARCH 11TH, 1942

Maronari related the final moments of the *Cygnet*, as seen from the deck of its attacker that night; "To the east, the shadows of the sunset already stretch to the ocean. Flaming clouds to the west swallow to last tendrils of gold. They move slowly driven by night breezes. In this wonderful play of light, sparkling on the trees and the tall lighthouse tower, *Cygnet*, the condemned vessel, still shows, emerging from the lazy waves. Suddenly the sky darkens. A red glow, followed by a piercing roar, breaks the flow of our thoughts. *Cygnet* has jumped into the air, water has invaded the boilers, causing the explosion and then the greedy ocean swallows another 4,784 tons" [he has over-estimated her tonnage by roughly 1,500, a non-uncommon practice].

Though the distance to San Salvador was less than six miles, it took the men some 10 hours to cover, by rowing, with little or no breeze to propel their sails. This was an average of about half a mile an hour. The locals were waiting, even though the survivors did not arrive at the dangerous reef line until 4 am. According to the Canadian Dods, a "Mr. A. B. Nairne, a one-legged American, who came out in a dory with two natives to lead the boats through the reef, had seen the sinking from the shore. The account of the attack was radioed [to Nassau] at once."

One can only imagine the surprise and joy of the crew at having a boat full of men risk their own safety to come out of the darkness through an opening in the reef to guide them ashore. There appears to have been some understandable confusion over who was a Nairne and who was one-legged. According to local sources, there were two Nairne brothers active in that part of San Salvador at the time, Emile and

Elmore. Both were described as "light-skinned" Bahamians and both had all their appendages. There was also a man named Thomas (Tom) Williams, a descendent of the British plantation-owning family which had lived on Sal Salvador since the 1780s, and whose patriarch was Burton Williams. Tom had lost a foot in a boating accident earlier on, and passed away in the 1950s. It is likely that a boat, sculled by Williams and carrying one or more of the Nairne brothers, came out to rescue the *Cygnet* men, and in the excitement the survivor, conflated their names.

Sofos' account is very much in accord with those of his shipmates. He relates, "The ship was sunk about five miles from the island of San Salvador, the first land that Christopher Columbus set his foot (in the new world). The weather was good, but there were groundswells in the sea. Around 8 pm we entered a cove, but as we were heading for the shore, our lifeboat hit a reef and water started gushing in. We immediately anchored, and using 5 buckets we started bailing out the water. The second lifeboat attempted to continue towards the shore to offload the men and return to pick us up. However, it proved impossible because the cove was packed with reefs which forced it to lay at anchor as well and wait for the daylight."

"When all the men had reached the point of exhaustion (thankfully, at least the temperature of the water was 82 [degrees Fahrenheit] and the morning breeze was neutralized by the exertion of bailing out the water) on the following day, Thursday, just before 4 am, a small boat appeared with two black men and a one-legged white man (who we found out later was the only white man on the

ATTACK, MARCH 11ᵀᴴ, 1942

island). We explained to them our predicament and we begged them to guide us to the shore as soon as possible, which they agreed to do. Our two life boats, following the small boat as a pilot, reached the shore around 5 am, thanking our lucky stars, because due to reefs, that cove was very dangerous and very rarely calm."

A local boy, about 10 years old at the time, "remembers hearing an explosion and waiting for word to reach them about what had happened. He also remembers the sailors being transported to town - an uncle or cousin had one of the few vehicles on the island at the time. He thought they came ashore at East Beach in two row boats. They were then shipped over to Nassau on the regular mail boat. ….he thought the ship was Dutch [it had been]. He remembers that the ship was carrying rubber, and that for a little while after the incident, large bales of rubber would wash ashore. People collected these and send them off to Nassau to sell."

Sofos describes how "when we reached the shore, we were led to the house of a native, just a few meters away, where we were treated to a cup of coffee. Meanwhile, they had called for transportation. A small truck came and, picking up 10 at a time, made 3 trips to transport all 30 of us to the other side of the island where the village was located. The village [Cockburn Town, on the west or sheltered side of the island] consisted of a few wooden houses, and the population of the whole island numbered about 300 inhabitants."

Nothing was spared for their comfort. "Our lodging was arranged in the church and the island administrator, an educated black man, extended a fine hospitality." This was

Hallam Reginald Ryan, the District Commissioner of San Salvador. Born in Port of Spain, Trinidad in January 1903, he was 39 at the time and had been a teacher and civil servant in Exuma prior to being assigned to San Salvador. Married to Marie, who was also from Trinidad, Ryanwas pensioned out of the Bahamian civil service inJune, 1955 at the age of 52.

Sofos continues that Ryan "....promptly telegraphed a list of our names to our New York office, as well as to the authorities of Nassau. He also gave us a detailed account of the events, because he had witnessed the whole drama of the attack and sinking of our ship, and as the island administrator, from the first moment (he became aware of the attack),he started sending S.O.S. hoping that an airplane from the American base would come and sink the submarine." Little did the participants know that the SOS was merely a whistle in the wind that there weren't the resources available at the time to traverse the Bahamas from Florida and counter-attack; there wasn't even a comprehension of the danger which the region was being subjected to by silent, largely invisible attackers.

To illustrate the point, an American sea captain who specialized in preparing privileged youths for college, Captain William M. Pond, and his wife were at that very time leading a troupe of students amongst the Bahama Islands aboard his schooner *Morning Star*. In a matter of weeks the word would get out, the yacht scurried into port in Miami, and most of the students enrolled in the US navy in order to fight the U-boat menace, which had come close to drowning them.

Chapter 6

SAN SALVADOR TO NASSAU, MARCH 12-13, 1942

Whether by the luck of good timing, or because the message was quickly sent from San Salvador to Nassau and a vessel immediately dispatched, the *Cygnet* crew were able to board the inter-island steamer *Monarch of Nassau* that very day. Sofos wrote, "finally, around 10 am of the same day, we boarded a ferry, the *Nassau Monarch*, and the next day, Friday, around 10 am we arrived at Nassau." Given that the distance from San Salvador to Nassau is roughly 200 nautical miles, the ship averaged 8.5 knots. They travelled in comfort, as the ship was fitted with 16 first class and 16 second class bunks and a state-of-the-art ventilation system.

SAN SALVADOR TO NASSAU, MARCH 12-13, 1942

The *Monarch of Nassau* in the builder's yard in Cheshire, UK, as the *Sir Charles Orr*, 1930. Captain Westmoredelivered her to Nassau in just 19 days.

Source: John Bowen, *Model Shipwright*, Number 90, December 1994, p. 58.

The *Monarch of Nassau* was built of steel as the *Sir Charles Orr* by J. Crighton & Co. Ltd., Cheshire, England, in 1930. Her dimensions were 90 tons, 116' in length, 21' in beam, 7.5' in draft, and capable of 11.5 knots when built. In the summer of 1930 she was delivered to the Bahamas from UK in a fast 19 days, from July 10th to 29th. This feat of seamanship, accomplished through several storms by Captain E. R. Westmore and six others, was so noteworthy that the story was published as far afield as Singapore. They returned via New York aboard the White Star liner *Arabic* to Liverpool on August 18th. In 1942 the ship's master is believed to have been Captain Roland Roberts of Eleuthera.

Named after Sir Charles William James Orr, Royal Governor between 1927 and 1932, the vessel was owned by Eleuthera Shipping Co. Ltd. and made fortnightly voyages between Miami, Nassau, and Eleuthera. Her maiden voyage to Miami was August 13th,1930,under a three-year mail contract for the colonial government. One of the lead shareholders was Major George R. Benson, Managing Director, along with other former military men who wanted to export pineapples and other goods from Eleuthera to Florida.

Founded by Sir George William Kelly Roberts (1906-1964), of Harbour Island, The "G. W. K. Roberts Co., also known as the Monarch Line, operated two small vessels, the 215-ton *Monarch of Nassau* and the 186-ton *Richard Campbell*, …these two were used on longer 12-day voyages through the Out Islands and usually called at the P&O Dock in Miami" (Kevin Griffin). In 1938,the *Monarch of Nassau* was disparagingly referred to, by a Miami reporter, as, "a prissy old tub with a hifalutin name." Late in 1939 John Hawes (*aka* Father Jerome, the Hermit of Cat Island, a Catholic priest and architect) sailed aboard her to his final redoubt, the Hermitage on Cat Island, at the highest point in the archipelago. During its exciting existence the *Monarch of Nassau* rescued a family of non-conformist self-styled Utopians who had travelled from California in the 1930s to "colonize" the Turks and Caicos with their own commune (it failed), traded bananas with the Greater Antilles, rammed and damaged a passenger ship named *Fire Island* in Miami, and was put up for sale in Texas. Its last Bahamian owner was Carl Sawyer.

The entire *Cygnet* crew arrived in Nassau at 10 am on Friday, March 13th the same day that a British steamer named the *Daytonian* met a fiery end at the hands of the *Tazzoli,* off of nearby Abaco Island. The *Cygnet*'s crew was only the second batch of survivors of submarine attack to arrive in Nassau, after the *O. A. Knudsen* less than a week before. The news was announced guardedly in the local papers thus: "Thirty officers and men from a freighter which was torpedoed in Bahamas waters Wednesday night are all safe and were landed in Nassau today. They are being taken care of by the Greek Consul and the Red Cross."

The Bahamian press had already dealt with censorship when in October 1940, British sailors Robert Tapscott and Wilbert "Roy" Widdicombe washed ashore on Eleuthera following a harrowing open boat voyage of 70 days and nearly 2,800 miles. The German raider *Widder* had savagely attacked their ship, the *Anglo-Saxon*, and they were the only survivors. The press then and in 1942 was torn between censorship, a duty to report the facts, and not wanting to miss out on the propaganda value of extolling the virtues of 255 buoyant merchant mariners who survived submarine attacks and landed on Nassau's doorstep.

Since concealing the survivor's arrival from townspeople was basically impossible (they landed in the centre of town), the editors of the Nassau *Guardian* and Nassau *Tribune* provided salient facts but concealed the names of ships and exact locales of the attacks. Later in the war they would quote from the more liberal US media in providing details of survivor's travails. By September 1942, however, there were no more survivors to report, as the Italians and their German counterparts had largely moved to other theatres, such as the bauxite route along the South American coast.

Chapter 7

NASSAU, MARCH 13-20, 1942

Gus Sofos was euphoric about his arrival in the capital of the colony, writing, "What a sight! What a surprise! The British authorities of Nassau, members of the Red Cross, and a large crowd of the town residents had flooded the waterfront." This included, perhaps surprisingly, the former King Edward VIII of England. He wife, Wallis Simpson, the Duchess of Windsor, personally greeted all 255 Allied survivors of submarine attacks who landed in Nassau during World War II. She did so in the capacity of the second President of the Red Cross, which was founded in the Bahamas by Lady Dundas, wife of the previous governor (who had been shipped off to Uganda to make way for the Windsors). Simpson's husband, HRH the Duke of Windsor, was Governor of the Bahamas between August 17th 1940 and March 16th 1945 the only British royal in modern history to hold a civilian job (it was his last).

NASSAU, MARCH 13-20, 1942

The Windsors were based in Government House in downtown Nassau through most of the war, though they enjoyed a peripatetic travel schedule to the US and Canada as well. Their presence not only uplifted the lives of Allied merchant sailors, for whom meeting the Duchess was something they all shared in common, but it also boosted tourism to the islands, helping to embuethe Bahamas with an aura of international glamour.

The Duke and Duchess of Windsor greet survivors of the Norwegian tanker *Kollskegg* at the Rozelda Hotel, Nassau, circa April 22nd 1942.

Source: "Survivors Meet Royalty Survivors of Sunken Ships Keep Duchess Busy," 23 April 1942, *San Antonio Express-News*, Texas

As head of the Bahamas Red Cross, the Duchess had her work cut out for her and a staff of nurses who drew their initial support from the Imperial Order of Daughters of the Empire. Three days after greeting the *Cygnet* men, she wrote to her beloved Aunt Bessie in the US: "we have been taking care of men landed here from three more ships a job for the Red Cross…" she was referring to the Norwegian survivors from the *O. A. Knudsen*, those from the *Cygnet*, and British survivors from the *Daytonian*. About the care of these vulnerable and often injured sailors Simpson would later write in her memoir, entitled, "*The Heart Has Its Reasons.*"

"A few months after Pearl Harbor, Nassau got its first real taste of the war. The U-boats suddenly appeared in the Caribbean and off the Florida coast, to prey on the tankers and ore boats coming up from South America. In the space of ten days five shipwrecked crews landed in Nassau. With the other ladies of the Red Cross, I did what I could to make them comfortable while they awaited evacuation. As that terrible spring wore on we began to receive some truly heart-wrenching cases men who had drifted for days without food or water under the searing tropical sun."

She concluded her letter by relating that "…I am endeavouring to open a canteen for the boys to keep them out of the grapevine! … We have just finished a Red Cross Fair in the garden [of Government House] and raised more than we expected thank goodness as the outfitting of these seamen is a drain on our resources…." She did ultimately, and against local opposition, open a canteen serving alcohol to servicemen and mariners. Her biographer, Michael Bloch, wrote, "The sight of the shipwrecked moved her to great compassion," ("*The Duke of Windsor's War.*") Certainly her work as principal care giver to the survivors lent an element of glamor to the otherwise pitiful conditions in which the men were rescued. Most of them spoke glowingly of their interactions, however brief, with she and the Duke.

Sofos continues, writing: "Once the formalities were completed, we were transported to the Hotel Imperial, which was owned by Mrs. Maillis (a Greek) from Kalymnos, where they served us coffee and sandwiches upon our arrival. Many of the Greeks (residents of Nassau) rushed to meet us and make our acquaintance, and the Red Cross distributed items of clothing [to each man]: a pair of shoes, a pair of socks, a set of underwear, a handkerchief, a shirt, a pair of pants, pyjamas, a razor, shaving cream, toothbrush, and toothpaste. We stayed in Nassau eight days, and during our stay our fellow Greeks, most of whom were from Kalymnos, extended such a warm and generous hospitality that it's impossible for me to describe, as it's equally impossible to describe our enthusiasm!"

In Nassau the officers and crew were well looked after by the local Greek community, which was led in part by Consul Christopher Esfakis, Acting Greek Vice-Consul, F. Scarlatos, and the Greek Orthodox Church, led by Father Spirtos. On the 18th of March, Captain Mamais filed a Letter of Protest, on the instructions of the owner, in which he "hereby gives notice of his intention of protesting" the sinking of his ship by enemy combatants. The Notary Public was Stafford Lofthouse Sands, Esq. (1913-1972), who later became a prominent politician and the Minister of Finance, later referred to as the 'Father of Tourism' in the colony.

Cygnet officers and crew being looked after by the Greek Orthodox priest, Father Spirtos, and members of Nassau's Greek community for a week in March 1942.

Source: Pericles Maillis, whose mother owned Imperial Hotel, where they had stayed.

On behalf of the Greek Line, the Halcyon Shipping Company appointed R. H. Curry and Company Limited of Nassau to be agents in the Bahamas. To handle the crew's needs and get them from Miami to New York, they used sub-agents Messrs., Albury, and Company of Nassau and Miami. The general manager suggested that the ship owners pay the Florida agents directly, "to avoid dollar exchange as there is considerable red tape in this connection." He also observed that the charity which the survivors were receiving was saving the owners money: "With regards to clothing for the men, the Red Cross and the Greek Community in the Bahamas have very generously assisted, and we do not think the men will need any more clothing."

During the seven days that the *Cygnet* crew laid over in Nassau they were joined by roughly 100 other shipwrecked mariners from the *O. A. Knudsen* sunk on 5th March, the *Daytonian* whose survivors arrived the 15th, and the *Athelqueen*. The Imperial Order of the Daughters of Empire (IODE) and the Red Cross scrambled to drum up funds, clothes, cigarettes, and basic amenities for the men. Local newspapers were filled with drives for supplies such as a refrigerator, fan, and cribbage sets, as well as listings of social events like movie screenings, dinners, dances, etc. to entertain them. Some of the men from other ships were taken into private homes, others were put up gratis at the local hotels, including the Lucerne, Rozelda, Windsor, Prince George, and Royal Victoria, and some of them had to stay in Nassau General Hospital. Captain Mamais submitted that at least four of his men had minor injuries. Given the crowding in local hotels from other survivors, most of the men would have stayed in private homes opened by members of the Greek community.

Mrs. Ypapanti Alexiou, a matriarch of the Greek community in Nassau recalled through Pericles Maillis: "...some were in bad shape, tired sun-burned, bruises, and minor wounds; talked about trouble with sharks. They were taken to the hospital for a couple of days; looked much better and rested after that. They were put up in an apartment, which the Greek Orthodox Church owned on Frederick Street near their house - near what is now the Central Bank. She was newly-wed and went with her husband and Father Spirtos to see them in the hospital. Her husband used to bring them to their restaurant Gleneagles to eat. They were in town for a couple of weeks, and then permission came for them to travel to USA. [She has] never seen or heard of [them] since. ...Other Greek families - Damianos, Maillis, Esfakis, Psilinakis, Mosko - all helped," (Maillis interview of Alexiou, March 30th, 2011).

An image of the Gleneagles Hotel and Restaurant owned by the Alexious in Nassau Bahamas in the 1940s.

Source: ebay.ie/itm/1940s-50s-Gleneagles-Guest-House-Nassau-Bahamas-brochure-/252311602887?hash=item3abef186c7:g:BB4AAOSw~OVWv~2j

NASSAU, MARCH 13-20, 1942

The Imperial Hotel, owned by Pericles John and Kalliope P. Maillis, on Bay Street, Nassau, taken during 1944, less than two years after the *Cygnet* men stayed there.

Source: Photo graciously shared by Pericles Maillis, son of the owners.

Captain Mamais published an open letter of thanks in the local paper the following day. It read: "The Captain, officers, and crew from the torpedoed Greek freighter who arrived in Nassau yesterday have asked us to express their deep appreciation for the kindness and hospitality extended to them by the Bahamas Red Cross, the Acting Greek Consul, the Greek community, and everyone else who helped. In asking us to express their thanks, they said 'Please make it very nice because everyone has been so kind and we cannot say how much we appreciate their goodness.'" The open letter of thanks was a genteel touch customary at the time. Because the *Cygnet* sailors were so heartily welcomed by the local Greek community, they largely stayed below the radar during their stay, in contrast so some of the sailors from other ships, who were the subject of local gossip.

Another view of the Imperial Hotel, the Maillis home, in Nassau, taken from the roof of the British Colonial Hotel, and showing the sponge trimming shed at rear. By 1942, sponging had largely died out, leaving the remaining Greek families to diversify into law, real estate, construction, hospitality and aggregates, among other industries. They remain integral to Nassau society.

Source: Pericles Maillis.

NASSAU, MARCH 13-20, 1942

There is a compelling back-story as to how a Greek widow ended up as den mother to several dozen compatriot sailors whilst war consumed their shared but distant homeland. According to her grandson, Pericles, the Imperial Hotel was built around 1922 and was "praised for the improvement to the area" in the local press. "When my grandfather realized he was going to die, he had my Grandmother and the five children sent to our ancestral Greek Island, Kalymnos, to be with family. He died in 1926, and my grandmother and the children returned to Nassau in 1929, after the great hurricane." (The hurricane devastated the islands' merchant fleet, and most likely necessitated the commissioning of the *Monarch of Nassau* that year). In order to get by, Mrs. Maillis converted the upstairs rooms of their home to rental apartments, one for her, and those later were absorbed into the hotel and even an al fresco nightclub.

As is usual when sailors or travellers lose their documents (they had to abandon their home in a matter of minutes, and most of them had only the shirt on their back), the sailors had to be issued new visas and passports. The American Consul, John W. Dye, worked closely with the agents and the owners to arrange these. Money was sent from New York for the captain to advance some funds to the crew. On March 17th, Dye telegrammed the Department of State requesting transit certificates for the "27 Greek, 1 Spanish, 1 Canadian, and 1 Rumanian seamen." The Greek Consul paid for the cost of the telegrams. At 7:57 pm on the 19th, "Welles, acting" for the US government granted the waivers. Perhaps surprisingly, given the speed with which they were forced to abandon ship, about half of the men were able to produce some form of identification.

Chapter 8

TRANSPORT TO MIAMI ANDNEW YORK, MARCH 21-23 1942

After exactly one week, on Friday, March 20th, the 30*Cygnet* officers and men secured passage on the inter-island motor vessel *Ena K.*, which provided a regular sea link from Nassau to Miami. It was a crowded voyage on the 12-passenger, locally built ship, as they were joined by two Bahamians - farm labourers, John J. Moss and Elisha Ferguson,as well as two survivors (injured gunner, Waldemar Lund, and Canadian Stewart Cameron) of the Norwegian tanker *O. A. Knudsen*, who were going to the Norwegian Trade Mission at 80 Broad Street, New York. Since there were a total of 34 passengers on board, nearly three times its capacity, several must have slept on deck, or rotated the use of bunks.

TRANSPORT TO MIAMI AND NEW YORK, MARCH 21-23 1942

Ena K. at the dock in Nassau, 1937. She carried roughly 200 Allied torpedo survivors from Nassau to Miami after periods of recuperation.

Source: Anne & Jim Lawlor, "*The Harbour Island Story*," p. 134.

The motor-schooner *Ena K.* served the Bahamas for 42 years, starting in 1927, when she was constructed of wood by Thomas Berlin Albury in Harbour Island, Eleuthera. She was named after a daughter of her owner, Trevor Kelly, a Nassau businessman who had begun a prosperous lumberyard on the capital's waterfront in 1920. Her dimensions were 87.5' long by 22.5' beam, 9' draft, was 116 tons burthen, and registered to Nassau. She replaced the *Isle of June* on the Miami-Nassau run, and performed three round trips a week. One of her captains was Charles A. Pettee. In 1930 her owners were first Mrs. Maggie A. Kelly of Nassau, and then, in 1942, the *Ena K.* Company Limited. Her agent was Albury & Co. The Nassau papers in spring 1942 made much of the *Ena K.*'s one-thousandth round trip between Miami and Nassau. By September 1942 Wallis Simpson wrote to her Aunt Bessie: "the two little boats are gasping for breath - leaping back and forth between Miami and here - and things are difficult to have." This was an acute problem for Simpson, who loathed flying after witnessing a number of air crashes whilst posted to an air base in Florida during her first marriage, and private yachts had been sequestered for the war.

According to author Kevin Griffin, one of "two little boats," the *Ena K.* could carry a dozen passengers and in January carried 15-year-old Sidney Poitier to Miami to live with his older brother. A round trip in the *Ena K.* cost $17.50, compared to $24.50 in the larger Canadian vessel, *New Northland,* before the war. The other was the 164-ton *Betty K.*, built in 1938 [named for another daughter]. Together they offered sailings in each direction every Sunday, Tuesday, and Thursday. Before the war, they had sailed from Miami at noon and from Nassau at 2 pm, but because of the exigencies of the conflict they moved back and forth as cargo offered, which would have been incessant, particularly before the new airfield was completed. During World War II *Ena K.* carried the officers and crew of *O. A. Knudsen*, *Cygnet, Kollskegg, Athelqueen,* and *Daytonian* to Miami.

The *Cygnet* sailors left at 7 am on Friday after the US State Department approved a visa waiver the night before. On the morning of the departures they were granted health clearance by surgeon Dr. A. Hugh Quackenbush. Originally from Montreal, he was employed by the Bahamas government since at least 1932. The US Vice Consul in

Nassau, John H. E. McAndrews, signed Quackenbush' affidavit on the departure. McAndrews was from Minnesota and based in London when he was appointed to Nassau on August 24th1939. He reported to Consul Dye, also of Minnesota. By 1947 he was living on Shirley Heights behind Nassau, and three years later he retired.

The *Ena K.*'s voyage to Miami covered roughly 200 nautical miles and took 17 hours at just below 10 knots. They arrived in Miami at noon on Saturday, the 21st of March. *Ena K.* tied up at the Clyde Mallory pier (Pier 2), on Biscayne Boulevard between Northeast 6th and 9th Streets. The Peninsular & Occidental (P&O) Steamship Company built the pier in 1912. The vessel's agents were Saunders & Mader, who had also represented the *Monarch of Nassau*. Ralph Saunders of that firm signed the inbound health certificate on the master's behalf. The immigration officer was C. S. Yeager.

Once cleared into the United States, the *Cygnet* men were taken to the United States Naval Reserve Armory at Northwest South River Drive. George Morrison, the British citizen of Romanian birth, was interviewed by Ensign A. T. Carter at 4:30 pm; then Lemos and Dods by Ensign E. L. Valier, USNR. Vlachakis was debriefed by Ensign Millard H. Shirley, and Falangas by Ensign George V. Salzer, Jr. The men stayed in Miami only a few hours before they entrained to New York. Sofos relates that members of the Red Cross took them to the Miami train station and ensured that they had sufficient food and drink for the trip. At the end of their travels they each hoped to be paid out and meet with the owner's representatives at 8-10 Bridge Street, Lower Manhattan, perhaps even to obtain their next assignment.

ERIC WIBERG

Bridge Street, Manhattan, in the 1930s, as it would have looked to the *Cygnet* officers and men when they visited the Greek Line there. Most of the war-era buildings have been replaced by high-rise office and condominium towers.

Photo: Author's collection, with thanks to Tom, bartender at the Whitehall Pub.

Sofos optimistically records that "We were picked by the Red Cross. In the evening we boarded the train for New York, where we arrived on Monday, March 23rd at 7 am. Since my permit to stay in the States as a seaman extended only to 2 months, I decided to apply for a legal entry permit. Mr. Eliopoulos took on my case for a $50 fee." This may have been Peter Arthur Eliopoulos, born in Sparta on August 15th 1879. Sixty-two years old at the time, he lived at 271 Third

Avenue. Then the *Cygnet* crew split off on different vessels from New York, scattering from union hiring halls in Manhattan to around the world, to continue supporting the Allied effort to keep beleaguered England and her Allies in the war.

Chapter 9

TAZZOLI, DAYTONIAN & ATHELQUEEN, MARCH 12-15 1942

Meanwhile the *Tazzoli* continued it deadly patrol. The next day Maronari observed, "It is 1:00 am. The sun sets behind the island of San Salvador by drawing an outline of fire with the profiles of the hills and coastline, sunk in the great light path, a long fiery black shape. ...the night has swallowed all the latest tendrils of gold. The air cools and suddenly a light breeze ruffles the surface of the sea, which has become grey. A pulsating light shines on the north coast of the island. The lighthouse of San Salvador works even in time of war? Is this an American joke? The night brings with it thoughts and reflections on the events. A quick review of that day allows us to rather lazily examine things and events, now routine for us.

In the control room, in the quiet shadows of blue lights, [Chief Engineer Franco] Firrao gossips with the lieutenant [Claudio Celli], who grumbles: 'Don't hit my head when you pass!'"If we have been seen from the shore, the better. That fills me with an intimate and profound joy... The wet berths welcome us and the lazy waves of the Atlantic gently lull the Corsair crew of the boat to sleep. The night passes, with every four hours the tranquil echo of the heavy tread on the guard plates above us...."

According to Mattesini, while Maronari was waxing poetic, di Cossato and his radio operators were trying unsuccessfully to communicate with Betasom officials in Bordeaux. On the 11th of March (the day of the *Cygnet* attack) Betasom ordered its Italian submarine fleet to cover the northern entrances to the Caribbean Sea the Windward, Mona, and Anegada passages, based on reports of Allied shipping activities there being filed by German U-boats. Since di Cossato was not able to establish communications with his base again until the 28th of March, by which time his low fuel necessitated a return to Europe, he opted to proceed northwards to the Northeast Providence Channel, between Abaco and Eleuthera. His intent at the time was to operate between Bermuda and the Bahamas, possibly off the northern coast of Florida, separated by less than 50 miles of Gulf Stream.

On the 13th, di Cossato found and sank the British tanker *Daytonian*, from which all but two of the men survived, and two days later another UK tanker the *Athelqueen* both east of Abaco's Hole in the Wall lighthouse. After sending a torpedo into the side of the latter ship, *Tazzo*li was not idle, and neither were the *Athelqueen*'s gunners. At 2:58 pm, or 20 minutes after the initial torpedo attack, the submarine surfaced on the starboard quarter roughly 2,000 yards away.

The gunners were ready, and Marine Gun-layer V. L. Coleman promptly opened fire with the 4.7-inch gun, which he had loaded in preparation for just such an opportunity. Captain Roberts was later to commend Coleman for not waiting for orders, noting: "The ship was down by the stern, making it very difficult to get a foothold on the sloping deck and fire accurately. However these shots made the submarine crash dive." As an indirect result of his action, Coleman put one of the deadliest submarines in the region out of commission for a patrol, which had claimed over half a dozen ships in just 10 days.

Realizing that it was being fired on (though all three shots missed), the *Tazzoli* crash-dived to avoid being hit. Di Cossato wrote in the log that the sub surfaced at [2:58 pm local time], "but noticing that the tanker's stern gun is ready to fire, we dive and surface again" at 3:34 pm 36 minutes later. Crucially, di Cossato by his own admission did not judge its distance from the ship or the submarine's forward momentum correctly. The *Tazzoli* collided with the middle of the starboard side of the sinking ship, badly damaging its bows and putting the forward torpedo tubes out of commission. Maronari observed that di "Cossato miscalculated the distance and when he tried to take another peek with the periscope, he still had not crossed to the other side and sighted the enemy ship so close that he could distinguish the bolts on the hull. The submarine tried to go deeper but seconds later, there was a shock and the submarine had obviously collided with the enemy ship."

Moronari reported that a powerful jolt forced the crew to tumble, and a cry went out: "What happened over there?"

TAZZOLI, DAYTONIAN & ATHELQUEEN, MARCH 12-15 1942

After a pause came the reply, "All normal," to which di Cossato mumbled "Thank goodness," accompanied by a great sigh. Di Cossato took the submarine to 132 feet to test the vessel's seaworthiness. No water leak was reported and everything appeared under control. "*Tazzoli* surfaced and it was observed that the bow was smashed to a length of three meters and the torpedo tube doors were apparently deformed and no longer usable." As Maronari wryly observed, the sentiment on board was, "We'll see later." Meanwhile, they had a sinking ship to contend with and put out of its misery.

The destruction of the British tanker *Athelqueen*, which caused damage to *Tazzoli*, effectively putting an end to its mission. As seen from the deck of the *Tazzoli*.

Source: Francesco Mattesini, "*Attack of the Betasom Submarines*," 2014

SWAN SINKS

Tazzoli's damaged bow following its collision with the *Athelqueen* off Abaco.

Source: freepages.family.rootsweb.ancestry.com/~treevecwll/athelqueen2.htm

It was a devastating end to one of the most aggressive patrols of the war. The *Tazzoli* was to see a number of otherwise easy prey fall by the wayside unharmed as a result of Coleman's bravery. There is no record that the men on the ship felt it lurch due to the collision, as they were occupied with saving themselves. While the submariners licked their wounds and checked frantically for any signs of water ingress, the men on the *Athelqueen* had bought some time though not much - to abandon ship in an orderly fashion.

Soon the *Tazzoli* re-surfaced and the men from the Italian crew frantically ran forward to assess the damage to the bow and report back to their anxious skipper. From Captain Roberts' perspective, the submarine "...surfaced ahead and lay there, knowing that we had no guns forward with which to attack. I realized that she was waiting for us to abandon ship and therefore gave orders to lower the boats." At the same time Maronari noted: "Tubes III and IV were ready, but it was observed that the enemy crew was lowering a boat and moving very calmly to evacuate. In these conditions, firing another torpedo could have caused butchery. It appears that di Cossato wanted to move his submarine ahead of the enemy ship to attack from the opposite side" and be outside the field of fire of the enemy gun crew aft. Historian Platon Alexiades noted: "probably di Cossato hoped to surprise the enemy gun crew or perhaps fire his torpedo on a side where there was no lifeboat being lowered."

According to Roberts, all 50 men abandoned the ship in the three operative lifeboats at 3:15 pm. The gunners snuck a working Lewis machine gun on board their boat as well. As the men rowed away from their mother ship, Roberts noticed from the Plimsoll line that the *Athelqueen* seemed to be levelling off. He wrote, "...I thought that within an hour we should be able to re-board her if the submarine did not interfere." As the men pulled clear, di Cossato began circling the *Athelqueen*, his men firing into it with their deck guns. Seven minutes elapsed between re-surfacing at 3:34 pm and when they opened fire at 3:41 pm. The British crew counted between 40 to 60 shells fired, mostly at the super-structure, which was still above water (in reality there were 128 shells fired - the confusion may stem from the fact that more than one gun was fired). Roberts noted: "...the submarine did not seem to be concerned about how many rounds they fired. I counted 60 rounds from her guns until finally I saw my ship sink."

Maronari was on deck at the conning tower of the *Tazzoli* and recounted the final minutes of the *Athelqueen* thus: "Both deck guns were manned and they opened fire delivering quickly some 128 rounds and the merchant ship was engulfed with fire. Apparently the reserve ammunition on her stern was hit and started a firework display, forcing the submarine to move away by a few hundred meters, but this explosion was apparently the *coup de grace,* and the ship took a heavy starboard list and settled... The water around her was covered with fuel, oil, and debris."

Maronari was characteristically poetic, describing how the air whistled with tracers and exploding ammunition. Di Cossato fired the final torpedo from the sub's stern tubes and *Athelqueen*'s stern swerved to starboard. According to Maronari, the ship's bow, "salt encrusted and covered with algae, thrust upwards with halyards pointing skyward. ...There was a horrendous roar of torn sheet metal," he wrote. "Pieces of scrap jumped into the air, then the boilers exploded and the ship disappeared into a massive gorge in the water. The water swirled for a long time, spewing forth oil, naphtha, and other wreckage. Then the water slowly calmed and silently closed forever over the tanker." The *Athelqueen* lies to this day in 14,692 feet of water. The submarine crew hoisted the sixth and final victory pennant for the mission.

Di Cossato, the "mousy-coloured" commander of the *Tazzoli*, after a patrol.

Source: piombino-storia.blogspot.com/2010/09/capitano-carlo-fecia-di-cossato.html

After the *Athelqueen* sank, di Cossato took his submarine amongst the survivors' boats to ask questions. Captain Roberts described his nemesis as "....mousy-coloured, very sun-burnt, and wearing a blue shirt with blue shorts. He spoke with a distinct German accent. I talked with the captain of the *Detonian* [sic] later, he said that the Captain of the submarine, which sank him, was an Italian and showed a large Italian flag. The submarines seemed much the same on comparison but we certainly saw nothing of a flag, neither

German nor Italian. The submarine looked clean and her nose appeared to be bent as if she had been diving in shallow water. The captain told us that we were 80 miles from land and then leisurely steamed off on the surface, apparently without a care in the world."

All was not well aboard the *Tazzoli*. The comparatively dampened reception they gave the *Athelqueen* survivors, compared with that given the *Cygnet* and *Daytonian* men, was because their own craft had been badly damaged. The crew knew that they were effectively out of the war for the next few months, except as observers, and ideally survivors. As a result, there was no jocular showing of the Italian flag after this attack. In his log, di Cossato identified his victim as the *Athelprince*, an English tanker of 8,782 tons. Since this was a sister-ship to the *Athelqueen*, he was near enough to the mark, but it illustrates that he was distracted, since he could have clearly learned the name of his quarry visually or by interrogation.

Di Cossato rather laconically noted in the log: "during the submerged attack we collided with the bow of the tanker. The resulting distortion to the bow damaged the forward tubes. When submerged we notice a leak in the port diesel room, and decided to return to base and not to use the two remaining torpedoes" the ones in the forward tubes which had been damaged. Overall, he had gone into the *Cygnet* attack with nine torpedoes and expended a total of seven of them on sinking three ships in five days. The remainder, however, were neutered. Having sunk the ship, and the men in the lifeboats having been interrogated, and bearing in mind that an SOS had been sent to and received by the Allies,

Tazzoli turned away from her week of conquests in the Bahamas.

While on the return voyage, knowing his weapon had been de-fanged, di Cossato drafted recommendations for awards for the men who had performed outstandingly during the action-filled patrol. For the silver medal he suggested First Lieutenant Gianfranco Gazzana Priaroggia, Chief Engineer Franco Firrao, and Lieutenant (junior grade) Claudio Celli. Weeks later, on 21 April 1942, Priaroggia was given his first command over the submarine *Archimede* and on 10 August 1942 that of *Leonardo da Vinci*, which was, with the *Tazzoli*, the top-scoring Italian submarine of the war. He was lost with *Da Vinci* in May 1943.

For the bronze medal he recommended Lieutenant (engineer) Michele Ferrente, Sub-lieutenant (engineer) Giuseppe Centelli, Navy Guard (or Midshipman) Vasco Pini, Chief Helmsman 2nd class Raffaele Montella, Chief Machinist 3rd class Arnaldo Pittini, Electrician's Mate 2nd class Nicola Manna, Gunner's Mate Pompeo Verna, Electrician's Mate 2nd class Giuseppe Kumar, Gunner's Mate Constantino Cecconi, and Helmsman's Mate Antonio Visicaro. On top of these recommendations, di Cossato submitted the participants in the sinking of 13 merchant ships and a warship for the bronze medal, and those that did not directly do so for the war cross of military valour.

Chapter 10

TAZZOLI RETURNS, SIX SHIPS SIGHTED, MARCH 16-31, 1942

During her voyage back across the Atlantic, di Cossato and his crewmates headed between Bermuda and the US coastline before turning east towards Europe. They are believed to have come closer to the United States than any other Italian submarine in either world war. During the voyage, *Tazzoli*'s men sighted six ships: the tanker *British Resolution* on the night of 16 March, an unknown tanker 2,500 meters away on the following morning, a neutral ship two hours later, the *Davila* on the 20th, an unknown ship on the evening of the 25th, and another three hours later.

In all cases the damage to the bow torpedoes and their tubes, coupled with a chronic shortage of fuel, prevented the attack. Nevertheless, the *British Resolution* and the *Davila* both reported seeing the *Tazzoli*, so the submarine's mere presence served the purpose of creating alarm among

TAZZOLI RETURNS, SIX SHIPS SIGHTED, MARCH 16-31, 1942

Allied bases, as well as resulted in the deployment of fruitless air and sea-borne resources. To the extent that an element of submarine tactics is to keep the enemy off guard, imbalanced, and unsure of where, when, and for how long to deploy resources, the diversion along the coast was effective even without firing a shot. In fact, even the Germans were confused.

The British steamship, *Davila* was unescorted and laden when the *Tazzoli* discovered her. The large submarine was limited to its deck guns. However, it had an advantage a surface speed as high as 18 knots more than its smaller German counterparts and much more than the plodding merchant ship. At 4:13 pm the submarine sighted the *Davila* on course 340 degrees north-northwest from a distance of 3,500 meters. Though di Cossato decided not to attack, he followed the ship just in case. Indeed, the Italians were spotted by their British quarry, which fought back.

Davila, built 1938, from the stern involved in a cargo operation.

Photo source: http://www.helderline.nl/tanker/185/davila/

According to Alexiades, the *Tazzoli*'s log reveals:"He had two torpedoes left but after the collision with *Athelqueen* he did not want to risk firing them, probably due to the deformation of the bows. He dived at 4:21 pm because the firing from *Davila* was becoming too close for comfort. The word di Cossato used is *pericoloso,* for dangerous. I do not know how many rounds of 100mm shells he had left, but he had already used nearly 200, so he may have been short on these too. He does state that he could not attack and altered course to 130 degrees. After being detected and fired upon, *Tazzoli* followed *Davila* from a submerged position. At 6:23 pm the sub again surfaced, then broke off, and followed its normal navigation back to Bordeaux."

At 10:48 am local time, the US Eastern Sea Frontier's Enemy Action Diary records an SSS message (for submarine sighted on the surface) from the *Davila*. The Italians also heard the British transmitting their SSS on 600-meter bandwidth, which enabled them to identify the *Davila* on their original patrol log.The War Diary of the US Naval Operating Base (NOB) in Bermuda for March 20th 1942 also verifies: "The day brought in two SSS messages. One received at 11:00 [am] was from the H.M.S. *Davil*a. A U.S. submarine, operating in the vicinity, was dispatched to the distress area." Amazingly the *Tazzoli* seems to have evaded detection not only by the US submarine sent to find it, but also three German submarines operating within 60 miles of the incident: U-123 under Reinhard Hardegen, U-105 under Heinrich Schuch, and U-160 under Georg Lassen. Though it was the closest to the position, U-105's commander does not record making an attack on a ship on the 20th of March 1942, and U-160 was too far away.

Hardegen, in U-123, one of the Aces of Operation Drumbeat, records in his patrol diary at 12 pm on the 20th that "Tanker DAVILA reports surfaced U-boat on the 600 meter frequency. Distance 60 miles. DAVILA reports that she is attacked by a U-boat. There are 2 to 3 emergency messages daily from tankers on the 600-meter frequency." Later, his men reported seeing a macabre sight: "...the bridge of a sunken ship drifts past. Possibly from DAVILA?" Indeed, the wreckage of the *Davila* might well have littered the North Atlantic that day, had the *Tazzoli* not been essentially limping home. *Tazzoli* was a proven war machine under an audacious and expert commander, making her a formidable adversary. *Davila* was fortunate to have entered and then sailed out of the periscope sites of the sub.

Without further noteworthy episodes *Tazzoli* arrived at the mouth of the Gironde estuary, France, on March 31st, culminating one of the most successful single missions to the region and of the war as a whole, with a ship attacked on the average every day of the week for a period of six days. *Tazzoli* spent April and May undergoing maintenance and repairs, and the crew rested.

Tazzoli returning from Bahamas to Bordeaux on 31 March 1942. Note the exuberant crew lining the conning tower and rails, the victory pennants including for *Cygnet*, as well as the damage clearly evident on the starboard bow.

Source: Achille Rastelli, "Carlo Fecia di Cossato," and betasom.it/forum/index.php?showtopic=28909&page=1

Another image of the ***Tazzoli***'s victory lap up the Gironde Estuary. A German naval pilot was on board to guide the submarine and a German naval escort vessel can be seen following behind, upper right. The Italian officers and crew could thus relax for the first time in months relief is clearly visible on this crew's face.

Source: Mattesini, marina.difesa.it/conosciamoci/editoria/bollettino/Documents/2014/Bollettino_2014

Chapter 11

DI COSSATO, CAREER & SUICIDE, FOLLOWING *TAZZOLI* LOSS

Tazzoli's next patrol would be to the Caribbean. But this time it would bypass the Bahamas in favour of a channel past Trinidad. She left port on the 18th of June and by the 2nd of August 1942 intercepted and sank the Greek *Kastor* near the equator. On the 6th, *Tazzoli* sank the Norwegian ship *Havsten*. Two men were taken prisoner. Following this success, the boat returned to France on the 5th of September. After having motored 10,348 miles over 71 days, two months of repairs in the naval yard were required. Di Cossato began his last patrol on the *Tazzoli* on the 14th of November 1942, bound for Brazil. On December 12th they intercepted and sank the British ship *Empire Hawk*, and possibly the Dutch ship, *Ombilin* (or *Sumatra*). On the 21st, the boat sank the British *Queen City*. On Christmas Day the crew found and sank the American *Dona Aurora* in the South Atlantic. Two of her crew were taken prisoner, and though seven died, 62 survived. It

DI COSSATO, CAREER & SUICIDE, FOLLOWING *TAZZOLI* LOSS

was to be the last ship sunk by *Tazzoli* under di Cossato. The submarine returned to Bordeaux on the 2nd of February 1943.

After roughly four years aboard submarines, di Cossato was transferred back to torpedo boats. He assumed command of the *Aliseo* in the Mediterranean. The *Tazzoli*, meanwhile, was stripped of its armament to enable it to serve as a supply boat to Japan. It left Bordeaux on the 16th of May 1943 loaded with 165 tons of material. The following day, communication with the submarine was lost. According to Cristiano d'Adamo, it is likely that the USS *Mackenzie* sank the submarine by a depth-charge attack on either the 16th or 22nd of May. Another possibility is that an aircraft sank it in the Bay of Biscay on the 16th.

All 66 or so of the officers and crew of the *Tazzoli* remain on eternal patrol.

di Cossato receiving a Knights Cross to the Iron Cross from Grand Admiral Karl Dönitz in Bordeaux for helping rescue 254 sailors from *Atlantis* and *Python*.

Source: modellismoallabuona.lefora.com/topic/3543669/Il-regalo-di-Giulio#.VygpqjArKUk

The loss of his former crewmates so soon after he left them made di Cossato distraught. He suffered severely from what might today be called survivor's guilt. Nevertheless, he again proved himself a dashing and capable commander when aboard the *Aliseo*, in an extremely fluid situation; in September 1943 he sank a number of German ships escaping the port of Bastia on the island of Corsica. However, he was overtaken by events larger than himself. The Royal Italian Navy surrendered, and as a consequence, officers were no longer required to swear allegiance to the king, but rather to the new government. Di Cossato could not accept those terms, and refused to serve. For this he was imprisoned and ignored.

The royal court in Naples also refused to receive him, though that was where he was being kept. To a man whose family had fought for noble causes for generations, for which his brother had perished, and whose busy life had been devoted to the same goals, it was too much for him to bear. Unable to reunite with his family in the north due to the fighting there, and unwilling to take up arms with the Allies against his former comrades again, he became deeply depressed.

In the upheaval of war and switching sides, authorities were unsure exactly what to do with di Cossato. In aletter to his mother dated August 21st 1944, he wrote, "For months I have been thinking about my sailors of the *Tazzoli* who are honourably on the bottom of the sea, and I think that my place is with them." Carlo Fecia di Cossato took his own life the day he wrote his final letter, which he ended with the instructions: "Hug Father and sisters, and to you, Mother, all of my deep, untouched love. In this moment, I feel very close to you and you all and I am sure that you will not condemn me."

His family had lost another son to war, and Italy had lost a military national treasure, who, like the namesake of his favourite submarine, had become a martyr. Over time the navy and the nation would come around, and recognize di Cossato in one of the highest ways possible, by naming a naval submarine for him. Generations of naval candidates, officers, and sailors would come to revere and repeat his name along marble hallways as well as steel corridors deep beneath the sea.

Chapter 12

POSTSCRIPT, FATES OF *CYGNET*'S OFFICERS, MEN & SHIPS

Captain John(Ioannis) Mamais married Kalliope (Kula) Louloudes, who was born in Andros in 1909 (she went on to live in Queens, New York, until June 2007 her mother's maiden name was Makrina). In January 1954 Captain Mamais was sailing as master of the Panamanian motor ship, *Enterprise,* between Yugoslavia and Texas. In 1955 he steamed into New York from Venezuela in command of the *Sunbeam*, and in 1956 he arrived in the US aboard the *Olympic Sky*. He appears to have had two sea-going brothers, Georgios and Demetrios.

Antonios (later Anthony) Eustratios Falangas ultimately parlayed the *Cygnet* sinking to immigrate to the United States, remaining in the country from his entry in Miami for the balance of his life. After taking a job as a clerk in a dry-goods store named George's Variety, in Somerville, Massachusetts, towards the end of the war, he married

Christine V., from Lynn, and they sold fruit in Saugus in 1945. Thereafter the Falangas' moved to Salem Street in Wakefield, outside Boston, became self-employed storekeepers, and raised a family. Falangasbecame a Mason in 1950, obtained a US passport in January 1952, and a naturalized American citizen on March 14th 1955. In November of 1956 he and Christine took their children, Elaine W. (Eleni, age 10) and Charles S.(Stratis, age 5), to Greece for four months aboard the liner *Olympia*.

Born the son of Eustratios (Stratis) in Stenies, Andros, on October 3rd 1911, he passed away in Charlotte County, Florida, on the 10th of February 1983, at age 71. His father Stratis, son of Nicholaos, and born in Stenies, in 1882, shipped to New York as Second Officer of the Greek ship *King Alexander* several times in the 1920s. Antonios' son, Charles Stratis, graduated from the Phillips Andover Academy in 1971 (where he played football alongside coach Bill Belichick of New England Patriots fame), and from Brown University in 1975. He and his wife Maura owned and managed the family's Montrose Drive-In Restaurant in Wakefield. They and his sister, Eleni, ultimately retired to Florida.

The Falangas family restaurant in Wakefield, Massachusetts.

Within a year of the *Cygnet* sinking, John Aeginitis (Eginitis) was serving aboard a ship named *Berthore*. In September of 1943 it appears that he was promoted to master, or captain, of the steam ship *Michigan*, flagged to Panama. In 1944 he was chief mate of the same ship, sailing between New York and London. A US citizen, he passed away in his native Greece in December 1996. Chief Engineer Constantinos Vlachakis was another Androsian, whose wife Maria waited out the war on Andros, where she was born in 1903. Afterwards, the Goulandris Brothers, through the Greek Line, was still looking after their officer. Maria Vlachakis immigrated to the US aboard the *Olympia*, arriving July 25th 1956 with their daughter Anastasia, 19, and son Constantinos, 10, along with 11 pieces of baggage. Their destination? Greek Lines' offices at 8-10 Bridge Street the same as for the *Cygnet* survivors 13 years earlier. The family had survived tumultuous times, with one record of their son Constantinos Jr. being deported with his mother from New York to Greece at age one-and-a-half aboard the *Nea Hellas* in May 1948.

Antonios Xanthos was born on Andros in 1903 and arrived in Boston aboard the Greek steamer *Andriotis* from the Ukraine in April 1937. He had joined in Andros as a sailor just weeks before. The previous year he had sailed from Rotterdam to Boston, arriving in January 1936 aboard the *Cape Corso*. In March of 1939 he arrived in Seattle from Cardiff aboard the *Frangoula B. Goulandris*. By May of 1943 Third Officer Dods had risen to master of the steam ship *Hastings*, sailing between Trinidad and New York. In October 1944 he was captain of the steamer*Felowcraft* between New York and Halifax. By April 1946 he was in command of the ship *Beresford Park* trading between Nova Scotia and New York, amongst other ports. In June of 1956, Dods was domiciled in Montreal and was appointed shore manager for the Great Lakes ship *Wahcondah*. The ship was sold in 1963. From at least 1965 to 1972 Dods was living in Vaudreuil-Soulanges, Quebec, and his occupation was listed as mariner, then the trail goes cold.

In April 1946, Leonidas Vlachopoulos returned to New York aboard the Greek ship *Kerkyra*. A decade later he returned aboard the ship *Tini*, and by 1957 he was still a pump-man on the same tanker, going to and from New York and Venezuela. In 1944,Leonidas Tsiridanakis of Crete was inbound to New York, aboard the *Nicolaou Maria* from Aruba. He immigrated to California, became a US citizen, and died in Greece in December 1980. Chief Steward Stylianos Kalogeras, from Chios, was sailing between France and New York in 1946 and appears to have settled in Ridgefield, New Jersey. He also served as an able-bodied seaman, and had a tattoo on his left arm.

Engine Trimmer Michael Brillis, of Chios, signed aboard the tanker *Pacific* shortly after the *Cygnet* episode, this time as an engine fireman, sailing between Aruba and Norfolk. He joined as Mike on the 16th of July 1942, and by February 1943 had transited the Panama Canal aboard the same ship.Fireman Michael W. Katradis was born in Chios in 1907.In 1943, he worked the steamer *Plymouth* between Trinidad and New York, andin 1944 was sailing aboard the ship *Cyrus H. K. Curtis* between the UK and New York. In June of that year he was aboard the ship *William Frew* between Baltimore and New York. The end of the war found him aboard the *Nathaniel Currier*, US-flag, plying between New Orleans, Tunisia, and Morocco. By late 1952, he was aboard the *Mission Purisima* between Japan and Hawaii. Katradis obtained his US citizenship in Ohio and passed away in Greece in May of 1973.

Radio Operator George (Giorgios)Lemos, had served as Second Officer under his relative Captain Dimitrios Lemos aboard the Greek ship,*Kyriakoula*between New York and the Caribbean in 1937 the Chief Officer was Panagos Pateras, also from a ship-owning family. In 1939, Lemos was Second Officer of the *Kalypso Vergotti*, between New York and Amsterdam. He was aboard the ship *Hellas,* between Quebec and New York, in 1948. Between 1955 and 1956 he was Chief Officer of the steamer *Taxiarchis,* between Japan, Oregon, and Europe.

Cook Athanasios Papathanasiou, was born in Athens, in 1899, and appears to have shuttled between New York and Piraeus to study between 1910 and 1915. He was 5'6" and 152 pounds, and in 1939 served aboard the *Nicolaos M. Embiricos* between Wales and New York. In 1947 he was serving as cook aboard the Panamanian ship *Pinta,* between France and New York, and in 1948 he arrived in New York aboard the *Anna N. Goulandris*. Interestingly, even this Athenian had an Androsian connection, as his wife Malpe hailed from Andros. Like Sofos he was only allowed eight weeks in the US after the *Cygnet* sinking, and is presumed to have gone back to sea shortly thereafter. Hegained US citizenship in New York on February 4th 1937 and passed away in Europe in October 1972.

Constantinos (Gus) Sofos was born on the island of Nisyros, Greece, in 1908. In May of 1945, before the war was over in Japan, he arrived in San Francisco, aboard the steamer *Cape San Martin,* from Honolulu, as a seaman, resident alien. With him were his parents, Nicolas and Calliope, who bore 13 children. His last permanent addresses were Woodside and Jamaica New York. In 1953, Gus, as he was known to family, was sailing aboard the *Strathport,* between Pusan, Korea, and Portland and Longview, on the US west coast, indicating that he was involved in the support of US forces in the Korean conflict. At 5'5" and weighing 150 pounds, he rose to the rank of Chief Engineer and became a naturalized American citizen in New York on the 26th of April 1949. In the 1950s he continued his seagoing career in Panama, Aruba, Yokohama, Los Angeles, Newfoundland, Singapore, Mexico, and beyond. When he passed in 1985 he was survived by his wife Mary and four children - Irene, Calliope, Joanne, and Nicholas - and several grandchildren. His son Nick is prominent in the Connecticut shipping community.

Ioannis Gavalas (aka John Gavallas), arrived in New York aboard the *Nea Hellas* with his younger brother, Nikitas, from Piraeus, in mid-October 1939, as a seaman. They listed Santorini, not Amorgos, as their birthplace. In October 1937, under the first name Ioannis (or Joannis), he sailed from Antwerp to Boston aboard the freighter *Tassos*, having signed aboard in Corfu that year. In April 1956 he served as a storekeeper on the *Olympia* from Piraeus to New York. In June of 1956 he was donkey man (deck engineer) aboard the Greek steamer *George D. Gratsos,* between Walvis Bay South Africa (now Namibia) and Baltimore. In March 1946 Gavalas sailed from the Philippines to New York aboard the

Greek ship *Hella*s. In ensuing years he called at Gibraltar, Montreal, South American and Caribbean ports. In a 1940 New York arrival document, he travelled with Ekaterina Coumentarou, presumably his wife. He had an older brother named Demetrios (like their father), who sailed to New York from Piraeusaboard the steamer *Byron* in August of 1928.

Engine room fireman Demetrios Skaltiotsis, was born on the 25th of March 1904, and thus celebrated his 28th birthday with his crewmates in New York two days after his arrival there. In December 1939, he was a fireman aboard the Greek freighter,*Nicolaou Georgios* between Buenos Aires and New Orleans, having signed on in Newcastle. In November 1940 he sailed aboard the *Marouka Pateras,* under Captain George Pateras, to Honolulu and then to Houston. 5'6" tall and 150 pounds, he had signed aboard in Le Havre, France, in April of that year. Skaltiotsis became a US citizen and passed away in his hometown of Athens in July of 1980.

Sailor Gerasimos Antzoulatos of Cephalonia, born on September 14, 1921, didn't waste time getting back to sea after the *Cygnet*. Less than half a year later he was aboard the Greek ship *Intrepido,* sailing between Trinidad and New York. He went on to marry Theodora (Lola) Pentelios, also of Cephalonia, born the same year as he, who lived until 2003. They had a son, Gerry (Gerasimos), on June 28th 1949, in Hermosa Beach, California, and another boy named Nikos. The son of Kate Mela and Gregorios, a farmer, Gerasimos (later Jerry) Antzoulatos passed away in Los Angeles on April 14th 1981.

Dimitrios Coukoulis (Koukoulis), born on Chios in 1904, was sailing aboard the US steamer *Medina,* in August 1944. He arrived from Tampico, Mexico in December that year as a 39-year-old, 5'7" tall and 175-pound, fireman. He was given a month's shore leave. It was a busy period for him, with voyages to and from Cuba, South Africa, Japan, Nigeria, France, the UK, and Morocco. The work as water tender and fireman must have been searing hot and draining for a man in his late forties. In November of 1956, there was a George Coukoulis managing the General Steam Navigation Limited of Greece, possibly a relation.

Fireman, Marinos VassilesTsilimos, was born on Chios on the 17th of July 1913, to Vassiles and Marcela Kalogera Tsilimas. In October 1945, he arrived in New York aboard the *James H. Kimball*, and in January 1946 returned there from Bordeaux, aboard the US steamer *Paul Bunyan*. In 1948 he served as fireman and water tender aboard the *Mormacstar,* between Canada and New York. By 1951 he was married to Evangelos, and living in Nikia, part of Piraeus. Standing 5'5" and weighing 150 pounds, he had brown hair and hazel eyes. He later arrived in Blaine, Washington aboard the steamship *Sea Mystery* as a seaman. In the post-war years his voyages took him to Yokohama, Los Angeles, New Guinea, Panama, and beyond. Issued US citizenship in Pennsylvania, he passed away in Greece on April 1st 1991.

Messboy George Morrison, 24, of Romania and the UK, and deck boy, Pio Arrizurieta, 29, of Orihuela, Spain, were both the lowest ranking and also the only non-Greek European sailors on board. George's brother was named Fiore and he was born in Socodor village, Transylvania. Pio's father was named Juan and his homeport, in 1942, was Balboa, or Bilbao, Spain. Bosun (Boatswain, or junior officer in charge of the deck) Michael (also Mihael Antonios) Douroudous was born on Hydra, Greece on September 1889. He registered for the US draft whilst based at 40 Madison Avenue, New York, in 1942. During this time he was married to Calliope, also of Hydra. Before he joined *Cygnet* he was unemployed and his closest contact was a friend name Antonio Zirbis at 52 Madison Avenue. He and sailor Michael Kritharis of Lemonia were the oldest men aboard the *Cygnet*. In February 1944 he was back at sea between New York, Boston, and Halifax, aboard the Panamanian ship, *Panchito*. In June 1950, he arrived in New York from Piraeus as a tourist aboard the *Nea Hellas*, alone.

Fireman, George (Georgios) Kondas, was born in Hydra, in about 1916, to Maria Kondas, who was living in Piraeus in 1942. Kondas had signed aboard in Liverpool. In 1955, he was fireman aboard the Greek ship *Evangelismos*, between Tokyo and Eureka, California, having signed aboard in Iraklion. This stint resulted in other voyages between the Orient and the west coast of the United States. In 1958, he was still on the same ship, en route in July, between Australia and Canada, via a bunkering stop in Hawaii. He signed aboard in Alexandria, Egypt. Kondas, immigrated to Melbourne via Freemantle after the war.

SailorStamaticos Kazacos, was born in Kavala, the son of Andreas, in 1914. Fireman Theodosios Nikolakakis, was born in Lavrila in 1913, to John, later of Athens. He stood 5'4" and weighed 142 pounds. Before joining *Cygnet* he was aboard another Greek Line ship, the *Orion*, arriving in New

York in March 1941 from Trinidad, then bound for Piraeus. Another of the Goulandris shipping companies is named Orion and Global.

Sailor Demetrios C. (Dimitrios) Bitros was a 5'7", 154-pound musician aboard the *Nea Hellas* when he arrived from Piraeus in October 1939, as war began to consume Europe, returning that December. He was born to Pericles in Piraeus in 1912. He had the same role in the same ship in July the following year, passing from neutral Lisbon to New York several times. After his *Cygnet* experience he was enlisted as a non-US-citizen, single, and without dependents. In February 1945, while living at East 90th Street in New York, he was rewarded with US citizenship. This musical sailor lived for over a century. Having been born days after the *Titanic* sank, in April 1912, he lived until late June 2013. After passing away in Brooklyn, Bitros, was buried in Calverton National Cemetery in New York.

Fireman Theodosios V. Denaxas, was born in Piraeus in 1904 and when the *Cygnet* sank, his wife, Fanni Denaxas, was living at Dervenakion 139 in that port. In January 1940, he arrived in Boston aboard the *Pantelis* from Glasgow, having signed articles in December 1939 in Dublin. In Liverpool in October 1940, he and a group of sailors and firemen shipped aboard the *Stylianos Chandris*, arriving in New York in March of 1941, after a stint as a greaser. Denaxas managed to obtain work with the Goulandris family on April 14th 1942, less than three weeks after returning to New York from the *Cygnet*. He shipped out to Chile aboard the *Ioannis Goulandris* and returned to the US at Wilmington, North Carolina, in September. A namesake of the ship's namesake, a

40-year-old second engineer, joined him on the voyage. At 5'4" and 140 pounds, with black hair and brown eyes, the 38-year-old Denaxas was slight for the hard labour that he endured, and must have been tough.

It is noteworthy that not one of Denaxas' 29 shipmates from the *Cygnet* opted to join him so quickly after their ordeal. On his next voyage, however, he sailed with *Cygnet* crewmate, Gerasimos Antzoulatos, aboard the Panamanian ship, *Intrepido,* between New York, Trinidad, and Jacksonville, returning on September 26th 1942. In 1945, he transited the Panama Canal aboard the *Intrepido*, and in 1956 arrived in Baltimore from Hamburg aboard the *Ivor Rita,* having signed the ship's articles in Rotterdam. By then he had risen to fourth engineer. In January of 1957, he arrived from Genoa at Port Everglades aboard the *Margarita Chandris,* this time as a donkeyman signed aboard in Naples.

Sailor Konstantinos (Constantinos) Tsiknas, was born in Syra in 1910 to Calliope, his mother, who was living in Athens when the *Cygnet* sank. He appears aboard the *Gerassimos Vergottis,* arriving in New York from Rotterdam in February 1939. In August of 1940, he returned to New York from Liverpool on the same ship. In December 1945, he returned from Antwerp aboard the US ship *William B. Travis,* as bosun (boatswain) with tattoos on his forearms. By 1949 the 5'7", 160-pound Tsiknas was granted a month's shore leave from the motor ship *Ocean Mariner,* which arrived in New York from Piraeus in late November. He had signed aboard in Newport News that September. A few months later, in January 1950, he sailed into New York from Istanbul aboard the same ship.

Engine trimmer Gregorios Yannakis was born on Tilos in the Dodecanese, near Turkey, in 1917, to his mother, Maria. His birthplace is also listed as Mandraki, the capital of Nisyros, between Tilos and Kos. In 1948, he was listed as single and based in Athens, and voyaged from Piraeus to New York aboard the *Marine Carp*, arriving in February.

On December 8th 1943 US military officials and the RAF reported *Ena K.,* from Nassau, to have been in distress 15 miles northwest of Bimini. Its lighting of flares, while it awaited a tow by a rescue vessel sent out from Miami, was mistaken for military activity. On October 8th 1964, the *Ena K.* was reported down-island in Dominica, offloading 10 tons of frozen fish and general cargo. In a 1968 legal case the *Ena K.* officers and crew were found negligent in towing a fishing vessel named *Tuna III* from Florida to the West Indies - it sank in the first hour. Then, on October 15th 1969, the 42-year-old vessel foundered east-southeast of Stirrup Cay Lighthouse in the Berry Islands, whilst en route between Grand Bahamas and Nassau with a cargo of lumber. The *Betty K.,* on the Miami-Nassau run, supplanted her. Having survived the war and then some two decades following it, the *Davila* arrived in Bilbao for scrapping on the 25th of January 1964. OwnerCarl Sawyer put the *Monarch of Nassau* up for sale in the US Gulf in 1951, and it is believed that she was taken there and scrapped soon thereafter.

Dr. A. Hugh Quackenbush was still in the Bahamas in 1954 over 25 years since he arrived from Canada, working at Thompson's Pharmacy on East Bay Street. He is remembered for leading a voyage on the mail boat,*Lady Cordeaux,*to Abaco, to treat residents devastated by the hurricane of 1932, and for being the first doctor at the death-bed of Sir Harry Oakes, following his yet-unsolved 1943 murder.

Constantinos (Gus) Sofos records that in December 1942, "By order of the INS [US Immigration and Naturalization Service], but moreover under pressure from the Greek Port Authority, I was forced to join the crew of S/S *Penelope*."

Goulandris Brothers fared better. The authors and academics, Ioannis Theotokas and Gelina Harlaftis, relate, "The activities of the Goulandris Bros. office, which developed during the interwar years, were continued independently from 1952 by Basil J. Goulandris (18861976) with his sons John and Constantine. With the traditional London office and Goulandris Brothers Hellas in Piraeus as its axes, the group of companies run by Basil and his sons was managing a fleet of 30 Liberties by 1958. The names of the company ships were all prefaced by the descriptor *Grecian*. By 1965, Goulandris Bros was managing a fleet of 27 ships, of an overall capacity of 300,000 dwt [deadweight, or cargo-carrying tons], and by 1975, the family fleet's capacity had reached more than 400,000 dwt. In the 1980s, Goulandris Bros continued managing bulk carriers. In the early 1990s, the grandsons of Basil J. Goulandris had taken up roles in the family business. From the 1990s to the present, the ...fleet managed by Goulandris Brothers has maintained the level of previous decades."

Back in Nassau, the Imperial Hotel was very famous for a time after the war as a nightclub when Pericles (Sr.) and Tony Maillis ran it. According to Pericles (Jr.), it was where cracked conch [now widely popular] was first marketed and Blind Blake, George Symonette, and Peanuts Taylor became famous Calypso singers. When the three Pericles boys returned from World War II, the Imperial Hotel was closed and the guest rooms converted back to apartments. Speaking of his grandmother, Pericles wrote: "she did a lot of good works for a struggling Greek widow living in Nassau during the war, with Greece overrun and universal suffering and three of her boys at war. She would have been right in the middle of Greek War Relief. We do know that once it became do-able, she vastly helped our starving relatives in the ancestral home with money and clothes, and later with a home and shelter for those coming to the New World and through to America."

CONCLUSION

What conclusions can we draw from an incident like the *Cygnet* sinking? As these words are written, the youngest of the Greek sailors, Gerasimos Antzoulatos, of Cephalonia, was aged 21 at the time. Born in 1921, he passed away at age 60 in 1981. Though I am still diligently trying to track down the men, the youngest would be 95 years old, and it would probably be best to let them pass in peace. So, as one generation passes, another is faced with documenting what happened, without live witnesses, but, if fortunate, with the help of surviving family members or archives. Some official correspondence, as in that of the Duke of Windsor to his bosses in London, have been scrubbed intentionally lost to history. Others little snippets of officialdom, photos, and seamen's books from the time still tell a lively story. And fortunately bombing during the war or since destroyed none of the records being sought.

Why has this story not been told? Obviously this was deemed a small theatre a backwater to the larger war being fought across the globe. However. the trade routes from Panama, the US Gulf, Caribbean, and South America which passed through the Bahamas', numerous deep channels were critical to the success of the overall Allied and Axis

CONCLUSION

missions, one to defend, the other to seek and destroy. Eventually the defenders became the destroyers, and half a dozen U-boats were sunk in and around the Bahamas and Windward Passage.

In my opinion, the main reason the story of the humble trampship, *Cygnet,* and other stories like it have not been told is simple, and encapsulated in one, important ethos of empire: prestige. I hypothesize that the British colonists were embarrassed by bedraggled, semi-naked, oil-soaked Allied sailors washing up on their shores without papers, without money, often starving, sunburned, cold, and scared. It dented the locals' carefully nurtured concept of the colonial overseers' racial, administrative, cultural, and military superiority. It exposed to Bahamians the stark fact that in early 1942 the Allies were losing the war on the waves, the war beneath the waves; that supplies were not reaching their destination, that beleaguered Great Britain could, indeed, fall. Even Churchill conceded privately that the U-boat menace was his greatest fear.

Although the district commissioner of San Salvador was able to activate an SOS message to his superiors, it elicited no military counter-attack, as Allied air cover over the Bahamas simply didn't yet exist until air bases were completed in the Bahamas later on. Nor were there any effective anti-submarine warfare defences at the time; the nearby Americans ignored hard-won British war experience, as well as their own bloody lessons from unrestricted submarine warfare in World War I in order to deploy virtually all their assets to avenge Pearl Harbor in the Pacific. Until they established hunter-killer aircraft carrier groups in mid-

Atlantic to very effectively destroy U-boats of both the supply and attack variety, they left behind outdated destroyers backed up by a coterie of amateur volunteers called the "hooligan navy" or "corsair fleet," to protect the coast. When mayors of coastal cities that relied on tourism stood up the military's request that they establish blackouts the government (amazingly) backed down until May of 1942.

Meanwhile, organizationally the Bahamas Islands, a British colony protected by the US military, were dissected by at least three sectors, in US Navy parlance, not all of them speaking fluidly to each other. In short, as the *Cygnet* and *O. A. Knudsen* sailors came to realize, the Allies in that region, and at that time, were not equipped to defend them, much less counter-attack the Axis prowling at will. Di Cassato and his shipmates exploited this reality to their full advantage by sinking two more ships in the Bahamas within five days.

As a general rule the remote communities of the Bahamian Out Islands, as they were known, had little contact with each other. I believe that the British, through censorship and by keeping the details of these attacks under wraps in archives in the UK and US, were quite content to let these heart-wrenching stories of survival remain untold. I posit that the home-spun rumours of Swedes or other alleged spies or German sympathizers accused of having sent messages to offshore U-boats and provided them with safe haven, food, water, and fuel (all of them false), actually do the Bahamian people and expatriates there a great disservice.

The injustice of these rumours is made all the more stinging when we peel back the long-dormant layers of

CONCLUSION

documentation to learn of the extraordinary lengths that so many people the Italians, Mr. Nairne, a fishing family which served 30 cups of coffee at sunrise, the US consuls, the Greek consul, Father Spirtos, the Greek community, hoteliers, restaurateurs, nurses, Red Cross volunteers, agents, anonymous donors of a wide range of materiel, captains Roberts and Pettee, Dr. Quackenbush, and innumerable others, including the Duchess of Windsor, the Imperial Order of the Daughters of Empire, theGoulandris ship owning family, and Mr. Eliopolous in New York went to in order to help the *Cygnet* sailors and their colleagues from other ships. That is the true story, and as modest as it may seem, it is an extraordinary one which brings great credit to Bahamians and expatriates alike the ruled and the rulers, from all walks of life, races, genders, and socio-economic backgrounds.

Of course, history has its own inexorable momentum. On July 10th 1973, the Bahamas became an independent Commonwealth nation; the ruled became the rulers. Though their national archives were, in 2009 when this research began, virtually barren of material on the First and Second World Wars, it could be found in the national archives of the US (in College Park, outside Washington) and the UK (in Kew, outside London), as well as Canada, Germany, etc. Over 75 years after these events, censorship has been lifted, allowing amateurs and historians to understand both sides of the conflict better, and with more perspective. The internet, with the easy availability of volunteer experts online, of genealogical, meteorological, and anecdotal biographical resources, detailed military databases, and huge troves of data, much of it previously unpublished, is of course an immeasurable resource, particularly as regards finding the families of survivors. So the story continues. And new generations assume responsibility for preserving and maintaining the many incidents and mementoes.

Ultimately the story of the *Tazzoli* versus the *Cygnet* is not about steel on steel, or about battle strategy. It is about more than the loss of 3,530 tons compared to roughly 20 million tons lost on all sides. It is an episode rich in human history and allegory. The vanquished, for one, became the victors the modest Greek seamen have had the last word. They lived to sail again. The humble *Athelqueen* effectively ended the *Tazzoli*'s war patrol not with gunshots, but with her slow-moving blunt steel sides, giving the aggressor an up-close view of her rivets.

When Antonios Falangas arrived in Miami from the *Cygnet* episode at noon on Saturday the 21st of March 1942, he was effectively immigrating to the United States. Years later his son-in-law asked him if he had made a success of himself. Falangas told the younger man to look around at his family's restaurant, the full till, the house he owned nearby, the car, the happy family, his son who attended a leading prep-school and an Ivy League college and replied, "Yes. I arrived here with fifteen dollars. Everything that I have earned beyond that is how I measure success."

In the eyes of history, Falangas and his fellow "swans" won, whether or not theirs was a small or substantial little battle in a larger war. The telling of the history of World War II, going forward, will be less about the great and powerful personalities and their massive battles. Those we know about already. Rather, future histories will be more

CONCLUSION

about individual stories, like the loss of the *Cygnet*, the unheralded ambitions of the *Tazzoli* and its commander. Every quilt begins with a single stitch, a single patch. This story is their contribution.

RESOURCES

Enrico Tazzoli & di Cossato:

Cristiano d'Adamo, regiamarina.net, Dame Siri Holm Lawson, warsailors.com, Platon Alexiades, "*Un Sommergibile non e Rientrato Alla Base*," or "the submarine which did not return to base," published by SB Saggi, Milan, in 1999 a first-hand memoir of crewman Antonio Maronari, in Italian. The *Survivors Statements* and crew list are from the National Archives and Records Administration (NARA) outside Washington, DC. Michael Constandy also discovered detailed US Immigration telegrams from US Consul, John Dye, to the State Department, regarding repatriation. Extensive details of the wartime and post-war movement of Capt. Mamais, Falangas, Third Officer William Forest Dods, Demetreos Vlachakis, and John (Yoannis, or Johny) Aiginitis (Eginitis) appear in ancestry.com. There is a useful board discussion there called "Falangas Family."

Local historian Pericles Maillis, kindly did the interview of Mrs. Ypapanti Alexiou, in Nassau on March 30th 2011. Dr. Thomas A. Rothfuss, then Executive Director of the Gerace Research Station on San Salvador, interviewed the (unnamed) local man who was witness to *Cygnet* survivors as

RESOURCES

a child. The background about the one-legged American comes from *Survivor Statements* and was corroborated by Dr. Rothfuss' witness. Details of Thomas Williams who "lost a foot in a boating accident and died about the same time that the U.S. military came to the use the island as a missile-tracking base in the 50's." appears at islands.thebahamian.com/ sansalvador.html. The primary resource for di Cossato's patrol in *Enrico Tazzoli* was "*Un Sommergibile non e Rientrato Alla Base,*" by Maronari, in Italian. The Greek Consul to the Bahamas, Gus Constantakis, was very helpful in looking through old records.

Cygnet, Monarch of Nassau, & Ena K.:

There were two articles in the local Nassau papers about the *Cygnet*: "Thanks So Very Much," a letter from Captain Mamais, in the Nassau *Tribune*, March 14th 1942 (page 1, lower right), and "Men from Torpedoed Freighter Land at Nassau," also Nassau *Tribune*, March 15th 1942. An article in the Charleston, South Carolina *Daily Mail*, of March 21st1942 is about the *Cygnet*reads "U-Boat Blasts Greek Vessel."

I found a brief citation from "*Schip en Werf*, Mei 1939, RDM collective Johan Journee" giving technical details of the *Mirach* which became the *Cygnet*. A history of RDM, or *Rotterdamsche Droogdok Maatschappij* (Rotterdam Drydock Company) is provided at Wikipedia.org. This cites a book named "*Schip en Werf,*" by Piet de Heer, TU Delft as well as wivonet.nl/nicopag2.htm. The history of the *Mirach* in the format standardized by the Dutch government records can be found at marhisdata.nl/printschip.php?id=4325.

Wrecksite.eu also has a detailed *Cygnet*page with photos. A lovely photo and technical details of the *Mirach* appears at shipmotiions.nl/RDM/RDM/RDM-061.html. My brother John and his wife Sofia Wiberg provided phone contacts for locals in San Salvador. On Newspaper archive.com I found several articles including "Survivors of Sub Attack are Landed," based on Associated Press wires on March 14th 1942 as well as "Unidentified Freighter is Sunk Near Bahamas," also by the AP. A short blurb in another paper, simply states "Sub Sinks Freighter," and yet another appears under the title "Enemy Subs Cruises Brazenly on Surface, Showing Lights." The *Lima News* of Ohio reported on March 15th 1942, about the *Cygnet* (unnamed) under "Axis U-Boats Renew Raids in U.S. Waters."

The search for details on the SS *Monarch of Nassau* took almost as much work as the *Cygnet*. It started with a legal citation in "Carl Sawyer, Inc. v. Poor Et. Al., the *Monarch of Nassau*, 180 F.2d 962 (5th Cir. 1950)" found on federalcircuits.vlex.com. Kendall Butler, historian, provided details of some of the Bahamian officers and crew. *Monarch of Nassau* appears in Fold3.com on March 20th 1944, being escorted with the *Richard Campbell* from Miami to Nassau, and on February 9th 1945, going from Port au Prince Haiti to Miami. A plan for the ship under its original name *Sir Charles Orr* was featured on the site modelboatmayhem.co.uk on the forums, October 2010. From that lead I was able to order, from the UK, *Model Shipwright Magazine*, December 1994 issue. This was the Holy Grail as it had an image of the vessel in the builder's dock as well as detailed specifications for modellers to work from, down to the gig, or boat.

RESOURCES

The Jamaican *Kingston Gleaner* of June 13th 1941 has an article on Rear Admiral John Scaife, OBE, entitled, "Naval Intelligence Officer Known Here Raised to Flag Rank." A list of Governors of the Bahamas at Wikipedia.org provides details of the tenure of Sir Charles William James Orr. Vesselindex.com provides the official number, as do crewlist.org.uk. The Singapore *Straits Times* of October 2nd 1930 offers an account of Captain E. R. Westmore's crossing to the Bahamas in its article "An Epic of the Atlantic Crossed in 19 Days by a 90-ton Model Vessel." The *Joplin Globe* of Missouri on April 14th 1940 tells of pilgrims being plucked from Inagua by the *Monarch of Nassau* after a failed settlement bid from California ("Group Disillusioned by Life on Island").

There were numerous references to the *Sir Charles Orr* and *Monarch of Nassau* in the shipping news columns of Miami newspapers, all found on newspaperarchive.com. An August 13, 1940 example is entitled, "New Boat Sails on its Maiden Trip Late Today." Rusty Bethel of Cherokee Sound wrote a memoir kindly shared by his daughter in which he cites early training on the *Monarch of Nassau,* between Nassau and Miami, as radio operator. (He later went on to help found ZNS, the national radio and TV station, in 1944 information provided by Capt. Paul Aranha). Finally, a Texas newspaper featured an ad for the sale of the *Monarch of Nassau* by name in the late 1950s, listing Carl Sawyer Steamship Agency in Miami as the seller.

APPENDICES

I: Original Crew List of the 30 merchant mariners and survivors of *Cygnet*, 1942.

#			S/M	Rank	Age	b.	
1	**Gavallas**	John	M	3rd Engineer	37	1905	Greek
2			M		37	19	
3			M		31	19	
4		John	M		31	19	
5			S		34	19	
6			M		49	19	
7	**Papathanasiou**	Athanasios	S	Cook	42	1900	Greek
8	**Skaltsiotis**	Demetreos	S	Fireman (Engine)	38	1904	Greek
9	**Antzoulatos**	Gerasimos	M	Sailor (Deck)	21	1921	Greek
10			S		29	19	
11			M		38	19	
12			M		29	19	
13			S		35	19	
14			S		23	19	
15			S		21	19	
16	**Morrison**	George	S	Messboy	24	1918	Romanian
17	**Vlachopoulos**	Leonidas	M	Chief Steward	33	1909	Greek
18	**Tsiridanakis**	Paulos	S	Sailor (Deck)	33	1909	Greek

APPENDICES

19	**Douroudous**	Michael	S	Boson (Boatswain - Deck)	52	1890	Greek
20	**Kondas**	George	S	Fireman (Engine)	26	1916	Greek
21	**Kazacos**	Stamatico	S	Sailor (Deck)	28	1914	Greek
22	**Nikolakakis**	Theodosios	S	Fireman (Engine)	28	1914	Greek
23	**Kritharis**	Michael	S	Sailor (Deck)	55	1887	Greek
24	**Sofos**	Constantinos	S	2nd Engineer	34	1908	Greek
25	**Bitros**	Demetreos	S	Sailor (Deck)	30	1912	Greek
26	**Denaxaz**	Theodosios	M	Fireman (Engine)	37	1905	Greek
27	**Dods**	William	S	3rd Officer	30	1912	Canadian
28	**Tsiknas**	Constantinos	M	Sailor (Deck)	32	1910	Greek
29	**Yannakis**	Gregorios	S	Trimmer (Engine)	25	1917	Greek
30	**Arrizulieta**	Pio	S	Deck Boy	29	1913	Spanish

| **Gavallas** | Amorgos | Athens | Father Demetrios Gavallas, Athens |

Papathanasiou	Athens	Piraeus	Wife Meipo Papathanasiou, Andros
Skaltsiotis	Athens	Athens	Mother Asimmina Skaltsioris, Athens
Antjoulatos	Cephalonia	Cephalonia	Father Gregorios Antsioulatos, Cephalania

ERIC WIBERG

Morrison	Comuna Scador Gudutal Arad, Romania	Comuna Scador Gutudal Arad, Romania	Brother Fiore Morrison
Vlachopoulos	Corfu	Piraeus	Wife Triantafilis Vlachopoulos, Piraeus
Tsiridanakis	Crete	Piraeus	Father Andreas Tsiridanaris, Pireaus
Douroudous	Hyrda	Piraeus	Wife Calliope Douroudous, Hydra
Kondas	Hyrda	Piraeus	Mother Maria Kondas, Piraeus
Kazacos	Kavalla	Chakida	Father Andreas Kazacos, Kavalla
Nikolakakis	Lavrila	Piraeus	Father John Niolakakis, Athens
Kritharis	Lemonia	Piraeus	Wife Stavrania Kritharis, Lemonia
Sofos	Nisyros	Piraeus	Father Nicholas Sofos, Caro (Greece)
Bitros	Piraeus	Piraeus	Father Pericles Bitros, Piraeus
Denaxaz	Piraeus	Piraeus	Wife Fannie Denaxas, Piraeus
Dods	Sudbury, Ontario, Can.	Middletown, Ont., Can.	Father Robert Dods, Middletown, Ont., Can.
Tsiknas	Syra	Syra	Mother Calliope Tsikanas, Athens
Yannakis	Tilos	Piraeus	Mother Maria Yannakis, Tilos
Arrizulieta	Yharraghuelua, Spain	Balboa, Spain	Father Juan Arrizubieta, Orihuela, Spain

II: Sixty officers and crew of the *Tazzoli* on her Bahamas patrol, Feb.-March 1942.

#	NAME		RANK	
1	**Allegrini**	Luigi	Torpedoman 2nd Class	War Cross of Military Valor
2	**Bignami**	Gino	Electrician	War Cross of Military Valor
3	**Boero**	Giovanni	Machinist 2nd Class	War Cross of Military Valor
4	**Bollero**	Mario	Stoker, Engine Room	War Cross of Military Valor
5	**Bontagnali**	Angelo	Petty Officer (Gunnery)	War Cross of Military Valor
6	**Borelli**	Pietro	Electrician	Bronze Medal
7	**Boscardin**	Enrico	Torpedoman	War Cross of Military Valor
8	**Botta**	Domenico	Petty Officer (Radio)	Bronze Medal
9	**Bottale**	Gustavo	Petty Officer (Engineer)	War Cross of Military Valor
10	**Brezza**	Giovanni	Gunner	War Cross of Military Valor

APPENDICES

11	**Cappetta**	Napoleone	Petty Officer (Electrician)	Bronze Medal
12	**Castiello**	Antonio	Sub-Quartermaster (Helmsman)	Bronze Medal
13	**Cecconi**	Costantino	Petty Officer (Engineer)	Bronze Medal & promotion for merit in wartime
14	**Celli**	Claudio	Lieutenant (Junior Grade)	Silver Medal
15	**Centelli**	Giuseppe	Midshipman (Navy Guard)	Bronze Medal demonstrating special courage & enthusiasm
16	**Corradi**	Sergio	Sub-Quartermaster (Helmsman)	Bronze Medal
17	**Cristofanini**	Guido	Petty Officer (Torpedoman)	Bronze Medal
18	**De Martino**	Gennaro	Gunner	War Cross of Military Valour
19	**Del Conte**	Limber	Signalman 2nd Class	War Cross of Military Valour
20	**di Cossato**	Carlo Fecia	Commander	Gold Medal for Military Valour, Silver Medal for Military Valour (twice), Knight's Cross of the Iron Cross (German)
21	**Di Sotto**	Francesco	Sailor	War Cross of Military Valour
22	**Dilda**	Italo	Sub-Quartermaster (Helmsman)	Bronze Medal
23	**Ferrante**	Michele	Sub-Lieutenant (Engineer)	Bronze Medal demonstrating special courage & enthusiasm
24	**Firrao**	Franco	Chief Engineer	Silver Medal
25	**Fornaciari**	Aldo	Petty Officer (Radio)	Bronze Medal
26	**Fornai**	Piero	Petty Officer (Gunnery)	Bronze Medal
27	**Furno**	Giuseppe	Electrician	War Cross of Military Valour
28	**Fusetti**	Celestino	Electrician	Bronze Medal
29	**Gazzana Priaroggia**	Gianfranco	First Lieutenant	Silver Medal
30	**Gelli**	Dario	Torpedoman	Bronze Medal
31	**Gianni**	Giovanni	Gunner	War Cross of Military Valour
32	**Giuntini**	Mario	Machinist 3rd Class	War Cross of Military Valour
33	**Guida**	Giusto	Petty Officer (Engineer)	Bronze Medal
34	**Interdonato**	Antonio	Sailor	Bronze Medal

SWAN SINKS

35	**Kumar**	Giuseppe	Electrician's Mate 2nd Class	Bronze Medal
36	**Leoni**	Mario	Radioman 2nd Class	War Cross of Military Valour
37	**Lombardo**	Angelo	Sub-Quartermaster (Helmsman)	Bronze Medal
38	**Lubrano**	Pasquale	Sailor	Bronze Medal
39	**Manna**	Nicola	Electrician's Mate 2nd Class	Bronze Medal
40	**Marega**	Mario	Stoker, Engine Room	Bronze Medal
41	**Montella**	Rafaele	Chief Helmsman 2nd Class	Bronze Medal
42	**Musico**	Santo	Petty Officer (Engineer)	War Cross of Military Valour
43	**Naccari**	Giuseppe	Petty Officer (Engineer)	Bronze Medal
44	**Natale**	Umberto	Sub-Quartermaster (Helmsman)	Bronze Medal
45	**Panni**	Duilio	Petty Officer (Torpedoman)	War Cross of Military Valour
46	**Passon**	Guerrino	Signalman	Bronze Medal
47	**Patane**	Giovanni	Petty Officer (Gunnery)	Bronze Medal
48	**Pezza**	Olivio	Stoker, Engine Room	War Cross of Military Valour
49	**Piscolla**	Vincenzo	Petty Officer (Radio)	Bronze Medal
50	**Pistoni**	Mario	Petty Officer (Gunnery)	War Cross of Military Valour
51	**Pittini**	Arnaldo	Chief Machinist 3rd Class	Bronze Medal
52	**Pizzignacco**	Luigi	Electrician	War Cross of Military Valour
53	**Righetti**	Aldo	Petty Officer (Torpedoman)	Bronze Medal
54	**Signore**	Pasquale	Petty Officer (Torpedoman)	Bronze Medal
55	**Tagliavini**	Antonio	Sub-Quartermaster (Helmsman)	Bronze Medal
56	**Tiozzo**	Luigi	Sub-Quartermaster (Helmsman)	Bronze Medal
57	**Toniolo**	Luigi	Petty Officer (Electrician)	Bronze Medal
58	**Verna**	Pompeo	Gunner's Mate	Bronze Medal
59	**Visicaro**	Antonio	Helmsman (Quartermaster)	Bronze Medal for exemplary, superior service
60	**Zingarello**	Michele	Sub-Quartermaster (Helmsman)	Bronze Medal

ACKNOWLEDGMENTS

The book is short and so is this list. I will only thank those that personally helped me. Most of those I owe credit to are featured in the Resources section above. Platon Alexiades, a Canadian-based author and research, deserves the most credit for sharing original Italian patrol records. On the ground in Nassau, Bahamas, three men were instrumental: Pericles Maillis, a volunteer historian of the vibrant Greek community there, Captain Paul Aranha, esteemed author, historian, entrepreneur and mentor who understands the islands from the air like no other, and Craig Symonette, who stems from a long line of industrious Bahamian businessmen, politicians, and most importantly shipbuilders.

One gentleman, Captain Makis Kourtesis, his wife Eleni, and son Michael, proved to be immensely generous of their time, welcoming me to their homes, first in Athens and then on the lovely island of Andros, in the Cyclades. Without them I would never have experienced the Captain's Village through the eyes of a fellow captain, and trodden down the same narrow whitewashed lanes that Captain Mamais, Falangas, and many others ran along, screaming with delight, as children. I was also able to wander the elegant and private

ACKNOWLEDGMENTS

lanes of Chora, the Port, or Owner's Village, and to appreciat first-hand the Maritime Museum of Andros, as well as a statu and park dedicated to the many merchant sailors who left thei beloved, spring-speckled island for sea during wartime, neve to return.

There has been a team of editors toiling away on thi and other books of mine in recent months, first in Arizona and Colorado, then in New Delhi, India. I am very grateful fo Aditi Ray B. for her exemplary copy editing, and to Sanchi Goel of PepperScript and his cover-design team for bringing all of this together in publishable form in short order. I thank my literary agent Alan Morell for his continued support without whose support team this book would not have been completed. I know they have my back.

For the identity of local vessels I also thank Kendal Butler, an expert in their history. On the ground in San Salvador Dr. Thomas A. Rothfuss provided exemplary local lore, proving that the sailors from the *Cygnet* impacted a wide range of citizens. As ever, the team at the Bahamas National Archives helpfully identified the District Commissioner of the time as well as other details. Every book especially those about local, as well as international history is very much a team effort. I am grateful to all friends, many of them made over this project, in Italy, the UK, Canada, the US, Bahamas, Greece, Norway and beyond, who speak many languages but share a common interest in preserving our past. And finally, to my parents, siblings, their spouses and children in the Bahamas and Sweden and my son, Felix.

ABOUT THE AUTHOR

Eric Wiberg has operated over 100 yachts over 75,000 nautical miles, many of them as captain. A licensed master since 1995, he is qualified as a maritime lawyer, and a long-time member of the Maritime Law Association of the US. He commercially operated nine tankers from Singapore for three years for the firm which lost the tanker *Braer*, and worked briefly for two salvage firms. He studied at five universities in three countries, including at Oxford. He has published six other books of nautical non-fiction. A citizen of US and Sweden who grew up in the Bahamas, he lives and writes in Westport, Connecticut and works in the shipping industry in New York City.

CPSIA information can be obtained
at www.ICGtesting.com
Printed in the USA
FSHW020918051020
74414FS

9 780984 399888